MANAGING GENETIC ANXIETY

Effective Approaches and Solutions

Shah Rukh

CONTENTS

CHAPTER 1: UNDERSTANDING GENETIC ANXIETY: A COMPREHENSIVE OVERVIEW

Introduction

Anxiety, a prevalent psychological phenomenon, has captured the interest of researchers and mental health professionals due to its intricate interplay of genetic and environmental factors. This chapter, "Understanding Genetic Anxiety: A Comprehensive Overview," delves into the genetic underpinnings of anxiety disorders, offering an in-depth exploration of their complexities and implications.

The Nature of Anxiety

Anxiety, characterized by excessive worry, fear, and apprehension, is a fundamental human response that has evolved as a survival mechanism. However, when it becomes chronic and disproportionate, it can lead to various anxiety disorders. These disorders, including generalized anxiety disorder, panic disorder, and social anxiety disorder, can significantly impact an individual's well-being and daily functioning.

Genetic Influences on Anxiety

The genetic basis of anxiety is a complex and multifaceted aspect of its etiology. Research has consistently shown that anxiety disorders tend to run in families, suggesting a hereditary component. The interaction between genetic predisposition and environmental factors further complicates the picture. Genetic studies, including twin and adoption studies, have provided insights into the heritability of anxiety disorders and the potential genes that play a role in their development.

Genetic Influences on Neural Circuits

The brain's intricate neural circuits are pivotal in understanding anxiety. Genetic variations can influence the structure and connectivity of key brain regions involved in anxiety regulation, such as the amygdala, prefrontal cortex, and hippocampus. These variations can impact fear processing, emotional regulation, and attention bias, all contributing to the development of anxiety disorders.

Neurotransmitter Pathways

Neurotransmitters are central to communication within the brain and play a crucial role in modulating emotional responses and cognitive functions. Genetic variations in genes related to neurotransmitter systems, such as serotonin, dopamine, and GABA, can affect an individual's susceptibility to anxiety. These variations can disrupt the delicate balance of neurotransmitter activity, leading to dysregulation of mood and anxiety.

Gene-Environment Interplay

The interplay between genes and the environment is a dynamic factor in the development of anxiety disorders. Genetic predispositions can interact with environmental stressors, such as early-life trauma and adverse experiences, to amplify the risk of anxiety. Epigenetic mechanisms, which modify gene expression without altering the underlying DNA sequence, further complicate this interplay. Environmental factors can trigger epigenetic changes that influence anxiety-related gene expression.

Developmental Trajectories

Anxiety disorders can manifest at different stages of life, and the genetic underpinnings play a role in shaping these developmental trajectories. Genetic factors can influence vulnerability during critical periods of brain development, hormonal fluctuations, and life transitions. Understanding how genes interact with developmental processes can shed light on the varying presentations of anxiety across different age groups.

Implications for Treatment and Prevention

Insights into the genetic foundations of anxiety hold promise for personalized treatment and prevention strategies. Understanding an individual's genetic predisposition could inform the selection of appropriate interventions. Pharmacological treatments targeting specific neurotransmitter systems or behavioral therapies addressing cognitive and emotional processes could be tailored based on genetic profiles. Early identification of genetic risk factors might enable proactive interventions to prevent or mitigate the onset of anxiety disorders.

Conclusion

The complexities of genetic anxiety are vast and interconnected, reflecting the intricate web of genetics, neural circuits, neurotransmitter systems, and environmental interactions. This chapter's comprehensive overview underscores the necessity of integrating genetic research with other domains of psychological science to fully grasp the origins and manifestations of anxiety disorders. Ultimately, this holistic understanding can pave the way for more effective interventions, improved diagnostic accuracy, and enhanced support for individuals grappling with the challenges of anxiety.

CHAPTER 2: UNRAVELING THE GENETIC ROOTS OF ANXIETY

Introduction

In the pursuit of comprehending the intricate mechanisms underlying anxiety disorders, researchers have embarked on a journey to unravel the genetic roots that contribute to their development. Chapter 2, titled "Unraveling the Genetic Roots of Anxiety," delves into the complex interplay between genetic factors, molecular pathways, and environmental influences that shape the landscape of anxiety-related conditions.

Genetic Predisposition: A Foundation for Anxiety

The chapter begins by illuminating the concept of genetic predisposition, which lays the foundation for anxiety susceptibility. Genetic studies, including twin and family research, have consistently indicated a higher risk of anxiety disorders among individuals with close relatives who also suffer from such conditions. This genetic predisposition forms the basis for further exploration into the specific genes and molecular pathways implicated in anxiety development.

Genome-Wide Exploration

Advancements in technology have allowed researchers to conduct genome-wide exploration, identifying specific genetic markers associated with anxiety. Genome-wide association studies (GWAS) have unveiled a myriad of candidate genes involved in neurotransmitter regulation, neuronal connectivity, and stress response. These discoveries contribute to a deeper understanding of how genetic variations can influence an individual's predisposition to anxiety disorders.

The Complexity of Genetic Variations

The chapter delves into the complexity of genetic variations that contribute to anxiety susceptibility. It explains the role of single nucleotide polymorphisms (SNPs), which are variations in a single DNA building block, in influencing an individual's risk of developing anxiety disorders. These SNPs can impact the functioning of neurotransmitter receptors, ion channels, and other molecular components critical to neural communication and emotional regulation.

Neurotransmitter Systems: Orchestrators of Anxiety

An in-depth exploration of neurotransmitter systems follows, highlighting their central role in orchestrating anxiety responses. The genetic roots of anxiety are intertwined with the serotonergic, dopaminergic, and GABAergic systems, which govern mood, reward, and inhibition, respectively. Genetic variations within these systems can tip the balance toward anxiety, leading to altered emotional processing and cognitive responses.

Epigenetics: Unveiling the Environmental Influence

The chapter delves into the intricate world of epigenetics, where environmental influences leave an indelible mark on gene expression patterns. DNA methylation and histone modifications are explained as mechanisms through which environmental factors, such as stress and early-life experiences, can modify gene activity. These epigenetic changes can influence anxiety susceptibility by altering the brain's response to stress and shaping emotional regulation.

Gene-Environment Interaction: An Intricate Dance

An exploration of gene-environment interaction unveils the intricate dance between genetic predisposition and external influences. The chapter elucidates how certain genetic variants can enhance an individual's vulnerability to environmental stressors, culminating in the onset of anxiety disorders. The interplay between genes and the environment creates a dynamic landscape where genetic predisposition amplifies the impact of adverse life events.

Emergence of Personalized Approaches

As the genetic roots of anxiety become clearer, the chapter underscores the emergence of personalized approaches to treatment and prevention. The concept of "precision psychiatry" is introduced, wherein genetic information guides the selection of interventions tailored to an individual's unique genetic profile. This approach holds promise for optimizing the effectiveness of treatments, minimizing adverse effects, and providing a more targeted response to anxiety-related conditions.

Conclusion

"Unraveling the Genetic Roots of Anxiety" concludes by emphasizing the profound impact of genetic research on understanding anxiety disorders. The chapter highlights the integration of genetic findings with neurobiological insights and environmental factors, fostering a holistic understanding of anxiety's origins. Through this comprehensive approach, researchers and clinicians are poised to transform the landscape of anxiety treatment, offering hope and relief to individuals affected by these complex and multifaceted conditions.

CHAPTER 3: THE INTERPLAY BETWEEN GENETICS AND ENVIRONMENT IN ANXIETY

Introduction

Anxiety, a multifaceted psychological phenomenon, is influenced by a complex interplay between genetics and environment. Chapter 3, titled "The Interplay Between Genetics and Environment in Anxiety," delves into the intricate dance between these two factors, exploring how genetic predispositions interact with environmental influences to shape the development and manifestation of anxiety disorders.

Genetic Predisposition: Laying the Foundation

The chapter commences by elucidating the role of genetic predisposition in anxiety development. Family, twin, and adoption studies have consistently demonstrated a hereditary component in anxiety disorders. Specific genes and genetic variations associated with vulnerability to anxiety are explored, emphasizing their potential to amplify an individual's susceptibility to environmental stressors.

Sensitivity to Environmental Cues

Understanding the impact of genetics on sensitivity to environmental cues is pivotal. Genetic factors can influence an individual's reactivity to stressors, shaping their propensity to perceive and respond to potential threats. This heightened sensitivity can lead to the development of anxiety disorders, particularly in individuals genetically predisposed to heightened stress responses.

Epigenetic Mechanisms: Bridging Genetics and Environment

A thorough exploration of epigenetic mechanisms follows,

showcasing their role as bridges connecting genetics and environment. DNA methylation, histone modifications, and non-coding RNA molecules are explained as key players in mediating how environmental factors, such as trauma or early-life experiences, can modify gene expression patterns. These epigenetic changes contribute to the lasting impact of environmental influences on anxiety susceptibility.

Stress as a Catalyst

Stress, a significant environmental factor, is intricately linked to anxiety. The chapter delves into how genetic variations can impact an individual's stress response systems, such as the hypothalamic-pituitary-adrenal (HPA) axis. Genetic predispositions can result in dysregulation of stress hormones, amplifying the impact of stressors and increasing the likelihood of anxiety disorders.

Gene-Environment Interaction Models

The chapter explores various gene-environment interaction models that elucidate how genetics and environment collaborate to shape anxiety outcomes. Diathesis-stress and differential susceptibility models are discussed, shedding light on how genetic predispositions can lead to both vulnerability and resilience depending on the environmental context. These models underscore the dynamic nature of the interplay between genetics and environment.

Neuroplasticity and Resilience

An exploration of neuroplasticity and resilience in the context of gene-environment interaction reveals the brain's remarkable adaptability. Genetic factors influence an individual's capacity to develop resilience in the face of adversity. The interplay between genes and the environment can influence neuroplasticity, enabling individuals to overcome challenges and mitigate the development of anxiety disorders.

Developmental Trajectories: Lifespan Perspective

The chapter extends the discussion to developmental trajectories, emphasizing the lifelong interplay between genetics and environment. Genetic influences can manifest differently across various stages of life, contributing to the emergence of anxiety disorders in childhood, adolescence, or adulthood. Environmental influences at each developmental stage interact with genetic predispositions, shaping anxiety-related outcomes.

Therapeutic Implications

Understanding the interplay between genetics and environment holds implications for therapeutic approaches. The chapter explores how this knowledge can inform targeted interventions that address both genetic vulnerabilities and environmental triggers. Personalized treatment plans that consider an individual's unique genetic profile and life experiences can optimize therapeutic outcomes, promoting recovery and resilience.

Conclusion

"The Interplay Between Genetics and Environment in Anxiety" concludes by highlighting the dynamic and intricate nature of anxiety's origins. The chapter underscores the need to view anxiety disorders through a comprehensive lens that integrates genetic predisposition, environmental influences, and their interactive dynamics. This holistic understanding paves the way for advancements in treatment strategies, prevention efforts, and the cultivation of resilience in individuals navigating the intricate interplay between their genes and the world around them.

CHAPTER 4: RECOGNIZING THE SIGNS AND SYMPTOMS OF GENETIC ANXIETY

Introduction

Identifying and understanding the signs and symptoms of genetic anxiety is crucial for timely diagnosis and effective intervention. Chapter 4, titled "Recognizing the Signs and Symptoms of Genetic Anxiety," delves into the intricate manifestations of anxiety disorders, highlighting how genetic predisposition interacts with environmental factors to shape the presentation of these conditions.

The Spectrum of Anxiety Disorders

The chapter begins by elucidating the diverse spectrum of anxiety disorders, encompassing generalized anxiety disorder, panic disorder, social anxiety disorder, specific phobias, and more. Each disorder is characterized by distinct patterns of excessive worry, fear, and avoidance behaviors that can significantly impair an individual's quality of life.

Genetic Vulnerabilities and Symptom Clusters

Exploring genetic vulnerabilities, the chapter delves into how certain genetic variations can influence the types of symptoms an individual experiences. For instance, genetic factors may predispose someone to experience more physical symptoms of anxiety, such as rapid heartbeat and trembling, while others might predominantly exhibit cognitive symptoms like intrusive thoughts and excessive rumination.

Early-Onset and Developmental Patterns

Recognizing the developmental patterns of genetic anxiety is pivotal. The chapter delves into how genetic predisposition can contribute to early-onset anxiety disorders in childhood, often characterized by separation anxiety or specific phobias. These early experiences can set the stage for the development of more complex anxiety disorders later in life, influenced by the interplay between genes and environment.

Co-Occurring Disorders and Comorbidities

An exploration of co-occurring disorders and comorbidities underscores the complexity of anxiety presentations. Genetic predisposition can increase the likelihood of anxiety disorders co-occurring with other conditions such as depression, obsessive-compulsive disorder, and substance use disorders. The chapter delves into how these interactions can complicate diagnosis and treatment planning.

Epigenetic Influences on Symptom Expression

Epigenetic influences on symptom expression are discussed, revealing how environmental factors can shape the way genetic vulnerabilities manifest. The chapter explains how epigenetic modifications can influence the severity and duration of symptoms, providing a nuanced understanding of the variability in anxiety presentations even among individuals with similar genetic predispositions.

Gender Differences and Cultural Influences

The chapter delves into gender differences and cultural influences that intersect with genetic anxiety. Genetics can interact with social and cultural factors to produce distinct symptom presentations. Understanding these intersections is pivotal in providing culturally sensitive and gender-informed diagnostic and treatment approaches.

Anxiety Across the Lifespan

Recognizing the changing face of anxiety across the lifespan is pivotal. The chapter explores how genetic predispositions can lead to different anxiety manifestations in childhood, adolescence, and adulthood. It underscores the importance of recognizing age-related variations in symptoms and adapting interventions accordingly.

Emerging Research and Diagnostic Tools

The chapter highlights emerging research and diagnostic tools that aid in recognizing genetic anxiety. Advances in neuroimaging, biomarkers, and genetic profiling are explored as potential tools for early identification and precision diagnosis. These tools hold promise for enhancing diagnostic accuracy and tailoring interventions.

Clinical Implications and Treatment Strategies

Understanding the nuanced manifestations of genetic anxiety holds clinical implications for treatment strategies. The chapter discusses how recognizing the genetic underpinnings of anxiety can inform personalized interventions. Cognitive-behavioral therapies, pharmacological treatments, and other therapeutic modalities can be adapted to address the specific symptom clusters and individual variations driven by genetic predisposition.

Conclusion

"Recognizing the Signs and Symptoms of Genetic Anxiety" concludes by emphasizing the importance of a comprehensive understanding of anxiety presentations. The chapter underscores that recognizing the interplay between genetics and environment enriches diagnostic accuracy, informs treatment planning, and supports individuals on their journey to managing and overcoming anxiety disorders.

CHAPTER 5: THE SCIENCE OF GENETICS: HOW ANXIETY IS INHERITED

Introduction

The inheritance of anxiety is a complex interplay of genetic factors that has intrigued scientists for decades. Chapter 5, titled "The Science of Genetics: How Anxiety Is Inherited," delves into the intricate mechanisms underlying the transmission of anxiety-related traits from one generation to the next. Through an exploration of genetic inheritance patterns, molecular mechanisms, and gene-environment interactions, this chapter sheds light on the scientific intricacies of anxiety's hereditary nature.

Mendelian Genetics: Unraveling the Basics

The chapter begins by introducing Mendelian genetics, the fundamental principles that govern how genetic traits are passed from parents to offspring. Concepts such as dominant and recessive alleles, genotype, and phenotype are elucidated to establish the groundwork for understanding the inheritance of anxiety-related traits.

Polygenic Inheritance: The Multifactorial Nature of Anxiety

The discussion then advances to polygenic inheritance, where multiple genes contribute to the inheritance of a trait. Anxiety disorders, being multifaceted conditions, often arise from the cumulative effects of numerous genetic variations. The chapter explores how the interaction of these multiple genetic factors can lead to a predisposition for anxiety disorders.

Heritability and Twin Studies

The chapter delves into heritability estimates and the insights gained from twin studies. These studies, which compare the concordance rates of anxiety disorders in identical and fraternal twins, provide valuable information about the role of genetics in anxiety inheritance. The concept of heritability is explained as a measure of the proportion of trait variation attributable to genetic factors.

Complex Genetics: Gene Variants and Risk Alleles

Exploring the complexity of anxiety inheritance, the chapter discusses specific gene variants and risk alleles associated with anxiety disorders. These genetic variations can confer susceptibility to anxiety by affecting neurotransmitter systems, stress response pathways, and neural circuits involved in emotion regulation. The chapter underscores how the interplay of various genetic factors contributes to the inheritance of anxiety-related traits.

Gene-Environment Interaction: Shaping the Outcome

An exploration of gene-environment interaction follows, highlighting how genetic predispositions interact with environmental factors to shape anxiety outcomes. The chapter delves into studies that elucidate how individuals with specific genetic profiles might be more sensitive or resistant to environmental stressors, ultimately influencing whether anxiety-related traits manifest.

Epigenetics: An Additional Layer of Complexity

Epigenetics is introduced as an additional layer of complexity in anxiety inheritance. DNA methylation, histone modifications, and non-coding RNAs are explained as mechanisms through which environmental factors can modify gene expression patterns, potentially increasing or decreasing the risk of anxiety disorders. The chapter underscores the role of epigenetics in mediating the interplay between genetics and environment.

Candidate Genes and Pathways

The chapter explores specific candidate genes and pathways

implicated in anxiety inheritance. Genetic variations in genes related to serotonin, dopamine, GABA, and other neurotransmitter systems are discussed in the context of their influence on anxiety-related traits. Molecular pathways involving neuroplasticity, fear conditioning, and stress responses are also examined.

Emerging Research and Future Directions

The chapter concludes by highlighting emerging research areas that continue to unravel the intricacies of anxiety inheritance. Epigenome-wide association studies (EWAS), gene expression profiling, and advances in computational genetics are introduced as promising avenues for deeper insights into the genetic underpinnings of anxiety disorders. These advances hold the potential to refine our understanding of anxiety inheritance and inform targeted interventions.

Conclusion

"The Science of Genetics: How Anxiety Is Inherited" concludes by emphasizing the multifaceted and dynamic nature of anxiety inheritance. The chapter underscores that anxiety's hereditary components are a result of intricate interactions between multiple genes, environmental factors, and epigenetic mechanisms. Through continued research and exploration, scientists are poised to further unveil the genetic tapestry that contributes to anxiety susceptibility, ultimately enhancing our ability to prevent, diagnose, and treat anxiety-related conditions.

CHAPTER 6: NATURE VS. NURTURE: GENETIC PREDISPOSITION AND ENVIRONMENTAL TRIGGERS

Introduction

The interplay between nature (genetic predisposition) and nurture (environmental triggers) is a central theme in understanding anxiety disorders. Chapter 6, titled "Nature vs. Nurture: Genetic Predisposition and Environmental Triggers," delves into the complex dynamics between genetic factors and environmental influences, exploring how these elements interact to shape the development and expression of anxiety-related conditions.

Genetic Predisposition: Laying the Foundation

The chapter begins by elucidating the genetic predisposition that lays the groundwork for anxiety susceptibility. Genes associated with neurotransmitter systems, neural circuits, and stress response play a pivotal role. These genetic factors set the stage for understanding how individuals inherit certain vulnerabilities that might contribute to anxiety disorders.

Environmental Triggers: Unveiling the Catalysts

Exploring environmental triggers, the chapter delves into how external factors can activate or exacerbate genetic predispositions for anxiety. Early-life experiences, traumatic events, chronic stress, and societal influences are discussed as catalysts that can interact with genetic vulnerabilities, tipping the balance toward anxiety disorders.

The Gene-Environment Interaction Paradigm

The gene-environment interaction paradigm is introduced as a framework to understand how genetic predisposition and environmental triggers collaborate to shape anxiety outcomes. The chapter explains how individuals with different genetic profiles might respond variably to the same environmental stressors, leading to distinct anxiety-related manifestations.

Epigenetics: The Bridge Between Nature and Nurture

Epigenetics emerges as a crucial bridge between nature and nurture. DNA methylation, histone modifications, and microRNAs are explored as mechanisms through which environmental factors can modify gene expression patterns. The chapter underscores that epigenetic changes can modulate the impact of genetic predisposition, revealing how nature and nurture intertwine.

Critical Periods and Developmental Sensitivity

An exploration of critical periods and developmental sensitivity follows, emphasizing how certain stages of life might be particularly susceptible to the interplay between genetic predisposition and environmental triggers. Childhood and adolescence, marked by heightened neural plasticity, are discussed as windows of opportunity for interventions that address both nature and nurture.

Resilience and Protective Factors

The chapter delves into the concept of resilience and protective factors that can mitigate the impact of genetic predisposition and environmental triggers. Social support, positive life experiences, and coping strategies are explored as factors that can buffer individuals against the development of anxiety disorders, illustrating the dynamic nature of the nature-nurture interplay.

Gene-Environment Correlation: A Bidirectional Influence

The bidirectional influence of gene-environment correlation is examined, emphasizing how genetic predisposition can lead individuals to seek out particular environments that align with their inherent traits. These environments, in turn, can either exacerbate or ameliorate anxiety-related vulnerabilities, showcasing the dynamic nature of the nature-nurture relationship.

Transgenerational Effects: Extending the Influence

Transgenerational effects are introduced as phenomena where environmental influences can impact not only the individual but also subsequent generations. The chapter explores how epigenetic modifications induced by environmental triggers can be inherited by offspring, potentially amplifying the transmission of anxiety-related vulnerabilities across generations.

Clinical Implications and Prevention Strategies

Understanding the intricate interplay between genetic predisposition and environmental triggers has profound clinical implications. The chapter discusses how this knowledge can guide the development of prevention strategies that target high-risk individuals. Early interventions, psychoeducation, and stress reduction techniques are explored as approaches that address both nature and nurture.

Conclusion

"**Nature vs. Nurture: Genetic Predisposition and Environmental Triggers**" concludes by highlighting the inseparable nature of genetic predisposition and environmental influences in shaping anxiety-related conditions. The chapter underscores that anxiety disorders are not solely products of genetics or environment but are emergent from the interplay between the two. This holistic understanding paves the way for interventions that target both genetic vulnerabilities and environmental triggers, ultimately providing a more comprehensive approach to managing and alleviating anxiety-related challenges.

CHAPTER 7: GENETIC TESTING FOR ANXIETY: BENEFITS AND LIMITATIONS

Introduction

Advancements in genetics have paved the way for the exploration of genetic testing as a tool for understanding and managing anxiety disorders. Chapter 7, titled "Genetic Testing for Anxiety: Benefits and Limitations," delves into the potential advantages and drawbacks of using genetic testing to identify genetic predispositions, predict risk, and guide interventions in the realm of anxiety-related conditions.

Genetic Testing: A Window into Genetic Predisposition

The chapter begins by elucidating the concept of genetic testing and its potential to provide insights into an individual's genetic predisposition for anxiety disorders. Genetic testing techniques, such as DNA sequencing and genotyping, are explained as tools that can identify specific genetic variations associated with anxiety susceptibility.

Personalized Risk Assessment

Exploring the benefits of genetic testing, the chapter delves into how it can enable personalized risk assessment. By analyzing an individual's genetic profile, clinicians can estimate their likelihood of developing anxiety disorders. This knowledge empowers individuals and healthcare professionals to tailor interventions and preventive strategies to address specific genetic vulnerabilities.

Informed Treatment Selection

The chapter discusses how genetic testing can inform treatment selection and enhance therapeutic outcomes. By identifying genetic variations that influence an individual's response to medications, clinicians can make more informed decisions about which pharmacological interventions are likely to be effective and which might lead to adverse effects.

Early Intervention and Prevention

Genetic testing's potential for early intervention and prevention is explored. Identifying genetic predispositions in individuals who have not yet developed symptoms allows for proactive measures to mitigate the risk of anxiety disorders. Psychoeducation, lifestyle adjustments, and targeted interventions can be initiated to address both genetic and environmental factors.

Ethical Considerations and Psychological Impact

The chapter acknowledges the ethical considerations associated with genetic testing for anxiety. The potential for psychological distress upon learning about one's genetic predisposition is discussed, as well as the importance of providing comprehensive genetic counseling to address concerns, manage expectations, and provide accurate information.

Complexity of Genetic Influence

The chapter delves into the limitations of genetic testing, highlighting the complex interplay of genetic factors and the multifactorial nature of anxiety disorders. Genetic variations might contribute only a fraction of the overall risk, while environmental factors, gene-environment interactions, and epigenetics also play pivotal roles.

False Positives and Negatives

The potential for false positives and false negatives in genetic testing is examined. Genetic variations associated with anxiety might not fully predict an individual's risk, leading to uncertainties in interpretation. Conversely, individuals with genetic predispositions might never develop anxiety disorders, raising questions about the clinical utility of such testing.

Population Diversity and Generalizability

The chapter emphasizes the importance of considering population diversity and generalizability when interpreting genetic testing results. Genetic associations identified in one population might not hold true for others due to genetic and environmental differences. This raises concerns about the applicability of genetic testing on a broader scale.

Integration with Clinical Practice

Exploring the integration of genetic testing into clinical practice, the chapter discusses the need for a multidisciplinary approach. Collaboration between geneticists, psychologists, and healthcare providers is highlighted as pivotal in ensuring the responsible and effective use of genetic testing for anxiety-related conditions.

Future Directions and Considerations

The chapter concludes by addressing future directions and considerations in the field of genetic testing for anxiety. Advances in technology, larger datasets, and more sophisticated analytical methods hold promise for improving the accuracy and predictive value of genetic testing. Ethical guidelines, informed consent, and education efforts are essential in navigating the evolving landscape of genetic testing.

Conclusion

"Genetic Testing for Anxiety: Benefits and Limitations" concludes by underscoring the potential and challenges of utilizing genetic testing in the realm of anxiety disorders. The chapter emphasizes that while genetic testing offers insights into genetic predispositions, it is just one piece of the complex puzzle that constitutes anxiety's etiology. A balanced understanding of the benefits and limitations of genetic testing is pivotal in harnessing its potential to enhance diagnosis, treatment, and prevention while ensuring ethical and responsible practice.

CHAPTER 8: BREAKING DOWN THE NEUROBIOLOGY OF GENETIC ANXIETY

Introduction

The neurobiology of anxiety is a labyrinth of intricate neural circuits, neurotransmitter systems, and genetic influences. Chapter 8, titled "Breaking Down the Neurobiology of Genetic Anxiety," delves into the complex web of brain structures, molecular pathways, and genetic factors that underlie the development and manifestation of anxiety disorders with a genetic basis.

The Brain's Fear Circuitry

The chapter begins by elucidating the brain's fear circuitry, which plays a central role in anxiety-related processes. The amygdala, prefrontal cortex, and hippocampus are explored as key players in emotional regulation, threat detection, and memory formation. Genetic variations can influence the functioning and connectivity of these regions, shaping an individual's propensity for anxiety.

Neurotransmitter Dynamics

An exploration of neurotransmitter dynamics follows, focusing on the role of neurotransmitters in anxiety modulation. Genetic influences on serotonin, dopamine, and GABA systems are discussed in the context of their impact on mood regulation, reward processing, and inhibition. The chapter underscores how genetic variations can disrupt the delicate balance of neurotransmitter activity, leading to anxiety-related symptoms.

The HPA Axis and Stress Response

The chapter delves into the hypothalamic-pituitary-adrenal

(HPA) axis and its role in the stress response. Genetic factors can influence the functioning of the HPA axis, affecting the release of stress hormones like cortisol. Dysregulation of this axis can amplify the physiological response to stressors, contributing to anxiety disorders.

Genes and Neural Plasticity

Exploring the role of genes in neural plasticity, the chapter discusses how genetic variations can impact the brain's ability to adapt and rewire itself in response to experiences. Synaptic plasticity, neurogenesis, and the role of brain-derived neurotrophic factor (BDNF) are explored as mechanisms through which genetic factors influence an individual's susceptibility to anxiety.

Fear Conditioning and Extinction

An exploration of fear conditioning and extinction mechanisms follows, highlighting the role of genetic factors in shaping fear responses and their extinction. Genetic variations can influence the strength and persistence of conditioned fear, contributing to the development of anxiety disorders. The chapter delves into how these genetic influences interact with environmental factors to drive anxiety-related behaviors.

Inflammatory Pathways and Immune Response

The chapter examines the relationship between genetic factors, inflammation, and the immune response in anxiety. Genetic variations can impact immune system functioning, contributing to chronic low-grade inflammation that is linked to anxiety disorders. The chapter underscores how the intricate interplay between genes, inflammation, and anxiety highlights the multifaceted nature of the neurobiology.

Epigenetics and Neurobiology

Epigenetic mechanisms are introduced as crucial mediators of the interplay between genetics and neurobiology. DNA methylation, histone modifications, and non-coding RNAs are discussed as epigenetic processes that can influence gene expression patterns in response to neural and environmental cues. The chapter underscores how epigenetics adds an additional layer of complexity to the neurobiological landscape of anxiety.

Neuroimaging and Genetic Markers

The chapter explores the role of neuroimaging techniques in identifying genetic markers associated with anxiety-related traits. Functional magnetic resonance imaging (fMRI) and positron emission tomography (PET) are discussed as tools that can illuminate how genetic variations influence brain activity and connectivity, providing insights into the neural underpinnings of anxiety disorders.

Translational Implications

The chapter concludes by discussing the translational implications of understanding the neurobiology of genetic anxiety. The insights gained from unraveling the neurobiological mechanisms can inform the development of novel interventions that target specific molecular pathways, neural circuits, and genetic factors. Ultimately, this knowledge holds promise for more precise and effective treatments for anxiety disorders.

Conclusion

"Breaking Down the Neurobiology of Genetic Anxiety" concludes by emphasizing the intricacies of anxiety's neurobiological underpinnings. The chapter underscores that genetic influences intersect with neural circuits, neurotransmitters, and molecular pathways to shape the development and expression of anxiety disorders. This holistic understanding enriches our grasp of anxiety's complexity and lays the foundation for innovative approaches to diagnosis, treatment, and prevention.

CHAPTER 9: COPING STRATEGIES FOR GENETIC ANXIETY: A HOLISTIC APPROACH

Introduction

Living with genetic anxiety requires a multifaceted approach that addresses not only genetic predisposition but also the intricate interplay of environmental triggers and individual coping mechanisms. Chapter 9, titled "Coping Strategies for Genetic Anxiety: A Holistic Approach," delves into the array of strategies that individuals can employ to navigate the challenges posed by genetic anxiety and enhance their well-being.

Understanding Genetic Anxiety

The chapter begins by emphasizing the importance of understanding one's genetic predisposition to anxiety. Awareness of genetic vulnerability can provide a foundation for exploring coping strategies that cater to individual needs and preferences.

Psychoeducation and Self-Awareness

Psychoeducation is introduced as a pivotal coping strategy. Understanding the biological basis of anxiety and the interaction between genes and environment can empower individuals to make informed choices and recognize that anxiety is not solely their fault.

Mindfulness and Meditation

The role of mindfulness and meditation in managing genetic anxiety is explored. These practices can foster present-moment awareness, reduce rumination, and alleviate the physiological and psychological responses associated with anxiety. The chapter underscores how mindfulness can complement genetic predisposition by promoting emotional regulation.

Cognitive-Behavioral Techniques

Cognitive-behavioral techniques are discussed as effective tools for managing anxiety symptoms. By identifying and challenging distorted thought patterns, individuals can develop healthier cognitive responses to stressors. The chapter highlights how these techniques can help modulate the impact of genetic predisposition on anxiety.

Stress Management and Resilience Building

The chapter explores stress management strategies and resilience-building techniques. Regular exercise, adequate sleep, and social support are discussed as factors that can buffer the effects of genetic predisposition and enhance an individual's capacity to cope with anxiety.

Healthy Lifestyle Modifications

Healthy lifestyle modifications, including balanced nutrition and avoiding substance abuse, are explored as means of nurturing overall well-being. These lifestyle choices can influence neurotransmitter functioning, hormonal balance, and inflammation, ultimately impacting anxiety-related outcomes.

Social Support Networks

The chapter delves into the role of social support networks in managing genetic anxiety. Connecting with friends, family, and support groups can provide validation, understanding, and a sense of belonging that counters the isolating effects of anxiety.

Therapeutic Interventions

The chapter discusses therapeutic interventions such as cognitive-behavioral therapy (CBT), exposure therapy, and acceptance and commitment therapy (ACT). These evidence-based approaches help individuals confront fears, develop adaptive coping strategies, and build resilience in the face of genetic predisposition.

Medication and Pharmacotherapy

The role of medication and pharmacotherapy in managing genetic anxiety is explored. Antidepressants and anti-anxiety medications can modulate neurotransmitter activity, offering relief from symptoms. However, the chapter emphasizes that medication should be used in conjunction with other coping strategies for holistic management.

Professional Guidance and Genetic Counseling

The importance of seeking professional guidance, including therapy and genetic counseling, is underscored. Therapists can provide tailored interventions that address the complex interplay between genetic predisposition and environmental triggers. Genetic counselors can offer personalized insights into genetic risk factors and their implications.

Creating a Coping Toolkit

The chapter concludes by emphasizing the creation of a personalized coping toolkit. Individuals are encouraged to combine various strategies, adapting them to different situations and stages of life. This toolkit can serve as a resource to navigate the challenges of genetic anxiety with resilience and empowerment.

Conclusion

"Coping Strategies for Genetic Anxiety: A Holistic Approach" concludes by highlighting the comprehensive nature of coping with genetic anxiety. The chapter underscores that genetic predisposition is just one element in the intricate web of anxiety's origins. By employing a multifaceted approach that integrates self-awareness, lifestyle modifications, therapeutic interventions, and professional guidance, individuals can navigate the complexities of genetic anxiety with a greater sense of control and well-being.

CHAPTER 10: LIFESTYLE MODIFICATIONS: NURTURING RESILIENCE AGAINST GENETIC PREDISPOSITION

Introduction

Lifestyle modifications play a pivotal role in nurturing resilience against genetic predisposition to anxiety disorders. Chapter 10, titled "Lifestyle Modifications: Nurturing Resilience Against Genetic Predisposition," delves into how adopting a holistic approach to lifestyle can enhance an individual's ability to navigate the challenges posed by genetic vulnerability, promote mental well-being, and mitigate the impact of anxiety-related symptoms.

Genetic Predisposition and Lifestyle Dynamics

The chapter begins by underscoring the influence of genetics on an individual's susceptibility to anxiety disorders. It emphasizes that lifestyle modifications can modulate the expression of genetic predisposition, highlighting the potential for resilience-building interventions.

Balanced Nutrition and Gut-Brain Axis

Exploring the impact of nutrition, the chapter discusses how a balanced diet rich in nutrients can positively affect brain health. The gut-brain axis is introduced as a bidirectional communication channel between the gut microbiota and the brain. Dietary choices that support a diverse gut microbiome can impact neurotransmitter production, inflammation, and mood regulation.

Regular Physical Activity

The role of regular physical activity in nurturing resilience is highlighted. Exercise promotes the release of endorphins, neurotransmitters that alleviate stress and anxiety. The chapter delves into how exercise influences neural plasticity and improves emotional regulation, counteracting genetic vulnerabilities.

Adequate Sleep Hygiene

The importance of sleep hygiene in managing genetic anxiety is discussed. Quality sleep contributes to neural restoration, emotional processing, and stress resilience. The chapter emphasizes that establishing healthy sleep habits can counteract the sleep disturbances often associated with anxiety disorders.

Stress Reduction Techniques

An exploration of stress reduction techniques follows, focusing on mindfulness, meditation, yoga, and deep breathing exercises. These practices can modulate the stress response, alleviate physiological arousal, and enhance emotional regulation, ultimately bolstering resilience against genetic predisposition.

Social Connections and Support

The chapter underscores the significance of social connections and support networks. Engaging in meaningful relationships can provide emotional validation, reduce feelings of isolation, and enhance coping mechanisms. The chapter discusses how social support can buffer the impact of genetic vulnerabilities.

Mind-Body Practices

Mind-body practices such as tai chi and qigong are explored as strategies that promote harmony between mental and physical well-being. These practices can foster relaxation, enhance self-awareness, and mitigate the physiological effects of anxiety-related genetic predisposition.

Avoiding Substance Abuse

The chapter delves into the impact of substance abuse on genetic anxiety. Alcohol and drugs can exacerbate anxiety symptoms, interact with neurotransmitter systems, and interfere with the effectiveness of coping strategies. Avoiding substance abuse is discussed as a protective measure to nurture resilience.

Cognitive Resilience and Positive Psychology

Cognitive resilience and positive psychology are introduced as approaches to cultivating a resilient mindset. Fostering self-compassion, cultivating gratitude, and reframing negative thoughts can counteract the cognitive biases associated with anxiety and enhance an individual's ability to cope with genetic predisposition.

Holistic Self-Care

The chapter concludes by emphasizing the holistic nature of lifestyle modifications. It underscores that resilience against genetic predisposition involves cultivating a balanced and comprehensive approach that addresses physical, emotional, social, and cognitive well-being.

Conclusion

"Lifestyle Modifications: Nurturing Resilience Against Genetic Predisposition" concludes by highlighting the potential for individuals to empower themselves in the face of genetic anxiety through intentional lifestyle choices. The chapter underscores that lifestyle modifications are not only about symptom management but also about fostering a sense of agency and well-being in individuals navigating the complexities of genetic predisposition.

CHAPTER 11: COGNITIVE BEHAVIORAL TECHNIQUES FOR MANAGING GENETIC ANXIETY

Introduction

Cognitive-behavioral techniques offer a powerful toolkit for managing genetic anxiety by addressing the thought patterns, behaviors, and emotional responses that contribute to anxiety disorders. Chapter 11, titled "Cognitive Behavioral Techniques for Managing Genetic Anxiety," delves into the array of evidence-based strategies that individuals can utilize to reframe their perceptions, build resilience, and alleviate the impact of genetic predisposition on anxiety-related symptoms.

Understanding Cognitive-Behavioral Techniques

The chapter begins by introducing cognitive-behavioral techniques and their foundational principles. It highlights how these techniques focus on the interplay between thoughts, emotions, and behaviors, aiming to modify maladaptive patterns and foster healthier coping mechanisms.

Cognitive Restructuring

Exploring cognitive restructuring, the chapter delves into how individuals can identify and challenge distorted thought patterns that contribute to anxiety. Techniques such as cognitive distortions identification, thought records, and cognitive reappraisal are discussed as ways to reframe negative thoughts and enhance emotional regulation.

Exposure Therapy

The role of exposure therapy in managing genetic anxiety is explored. This technique involves gradual exposure to anxiety-provoking situations, helping individuals confront their fears in a controlled manner. The chapter discusses how exposure therapy can desensitize individuals to triggers and weaken the association between genetic predisposition and anxiety responses.

Behavioral Activation

The chapter delves into behavioral activation, a technique that focuses on increasing engagement in positive and rewarding activities. By countering the avoidance behaviors often associated with anxiety, individuals can break the cycle of genetic predisposition leading to heightened anxiety responses.

Problem-Solving Skills

Problem-solving skills are discussed as tools to address situational stressors. The chapter explores how individuals can identify challenges, generate potential solutions, and implement effective strategies. Problem-solving skills enhance a sense of agency and control over genetic anxiety triggers.

Mindfulness and Acceptance

The integration of mindfulness and acceptance-based techniques is explored. Mindfulness fosters present-moment awareness, allowing individuals to observe their thoughts without judgment. Acceptance-based approaches encourage individuals to acknowledge their emotions and experiences, reducing the impact of genetic predisposition on anxiety.

Stress Management and Relaxation Techniques

The chapter delves into stress management and relaxation techniques. Progressive muscle relaxation, deep breathing exercises, and guided imagery are discussed as tools to alleviate physiological arousal and promote emotional calmness, countering the heightened stress response associated with genetic predisposition.

Assertiveness Training

Assertiveness training is introduced as a strategy to enhance communication and boundary-setting. Individuals can learn to express their needs and preferences effectively, reducing interpersonal stressors that might interact with genetic vulnerability to trigger anxiety.

Time Management and Goal Setting

The chapter discusses time management and goal-setting techniques. These strategies can enhance individuals' sense of control over their lives, reduce feelings of overwhelm, and prevent genetic predisposition from amplifying the impact of stressors.

Relapse Prevention and Long-Term Maintenance

The importance of relapse prevention and long-term maintenance of cognitive-behavioral techniques is emphasized. The chapter underscores the need to continually practice and refine these skills to ensure lasting resilience against genetic predisposition.

Conclusion

"Cognitive Behavioral Techniques for Managing Genetic Anxiety" concludes by highlighting the transformative potential of cognitive-behavioral techniques in the context of genetic anxiety. The chapter underscores that by actively engaging in these evidence-based strategies, individuals can reframe their relationship with anxiety, harness their innate resilience, and navigate the challenges posed by genetic predisposition with empowerment and efficacy.

CHAPTER 12: MINDFULNESS AND MEDITATION: CALMING THE ANXIOUS GENETIC MIND

Introduction

Mindfulness and meditation offer a profound approach to calming the anxious genetic mind by cultivating present-moment awareness, emotional regulation, and resilience. Chapter 12, titled "Mindfulness and Meditation: Calming the Anxious Genetic Mind," delves into the transformative power of mindfulness and meditation in managing the impact of genetic predisposition on anxiety-related symptoms.

Understanding Mindfulness and Meditation

The chapter begins by introducing mindfulness and meditation as practices that involve paying deliberate attention to the present moment. It underscores how these techniques can counteract the tendency of genetic anxiety to lead the mind into a spiral of worry and rumination.

Mindfulness: Cultivating Present-Moment Awareness

Exploring mindfulness, the chapter discusses how individuals can practice observing their thoughts, emotions, and bodily sensations without judgment. Mindfulness fosters awareness of the present moment, enabling individuals to detach from anxious thoughts linked to genetic predisposition.

Mindfulness-Based Stress Reduction (MBSR)

The role of Mindfulness-Based Stress Reduction (MBSR) is highlighted. MBSR is a structured program that incorporates mindfulness meditation, yoga, and self-awareness practices. The chapter discusses how MBSR can mitigate the physiological and psychological effects of genetic anxiety.

Meditation: Nurturing Emotional Regulation

An exploration of meditation follows, focusing on its role in nurturing emotional regulation. Meditation techniques such as loving-kindness meditation, body scan, and focused attention meditation are discussed as ways to cultivate compassion, reduce reactivity, and counteract genetic predisposition to heightened emotional responses.

Mindfulness and Neural Plasticity

The chapter delves into the relationship between mindfulness and neural plasticity. By engaging in regular mindfulness practice, individuals can reshape neural pathways and create new patterns of response to anxiety triggers, ultimately modulating the impact of genetic predisposition on anxiety.

Mindfulness-Based Cognitive Therapy (MBCT)

The integration of mindfulness with cognitive-behavioral principles is explored through Mindfulness-Based Cognitive Therapy (MBCT). This approach combines mindfulness practices with cognitive restructuring, empowering individuals to manage the cognitive aspects of genetic anxiety.

Mindfulness and Genetic Epigenetics

The chapter discusses the potential influence of mindfulness on genetic epigenetics. While research is ongoing, mindfulness is considered to impact gene expression through epigenetic mechanisms, potentially counteracting the expression of anxiety-related genes.

Neuroplastic Changes and Mindfulness

The chapter highlights neuroplastic changes induced by mindfulness practice. Neuroimaging studies suggest that mindfulness can strengthen brain regions associated with emotional regulation, attention control, and self-awareness, offering a protective buffer against the effects of genetic predisposition.

Mindfulness in Everyday Life

The integration of mindfulness into everyday life is discussed. The chapter explores how individuals can apply mindfulness principles to routine activities, enhancing their ability to stay present, manage stressors, and navigate the challenges of genetic anxiety.

Cultivating Resilience Through Mindfulness

The chapter concludes by emphasizing the role of mindfulness in cultivating resilience against genetic predisposition. It underscores how mindfulness empowers individuals to respond skillfully to anxiety triggers, develop greater self-compassion, and foster emotional balance.

Conclusion

"Mindfulness and Meditation: Calming the Anxious Genetic Mind" concludes by highlighting the potential for individuals to transform their relationship with genetic anxiety through mindfulness and meditation practices. The chapter underscores that these practices offer a means to create a sense of inner calm, tap into innate resilience, and transcend the limitations of genetic predisposition, ultimately fostering a state of well-being and self-mastery.

CHAPTER 13: THE ROLE OF NUTRITION IN ALLEVIATING GENETIC ANXIETY

Introduction

Nutrition plays a pivotal role in alleviating genetic anxiety by influencing neurotransmitter production, inflammation, and overall brain health. Chapter 13, titled "The Role of Nutrition in Alleviating Genetic Anxiety," delves into how dietary choices can modulate the impact of genetic predisposition on anxiety-related symptoms and promote emotional well-being.

Understanding the Gut-Brain Connection

The chapter begins by introducing the gut-brain connection and its relevance to anxiety. It emphasizes that the gut microbiome and its interactions with the brain can impact mood regulation, stress response, and genetic expression related to anxiety.

Neurotransmitters and Nutritional Precursors

Exploring the relationship between nutrition and neurotransmitters, the chapter discusses how certain nutrients serve as precursors for neurotransmitter synthesis. Amino acids like tryptophan, tyrosine, and glutamine are explored in the context of their role in producing serotonin, dopamine, and GABA - neurotransmitters that play a vital role in anxiety modulation.

Omega-3 Fatty Acids and Brain Health

The role of omega-3 fatty acids in brain health is highlighted. These essential fats have anti-inflammatory properties and can influence neural plasticity, potentially counteracting the effects of genetic predisposition on anxiety and promoting cognitive resilience.

Micronutrients and Vitamins

Exploring the impact of micronutrients and vitamins, the chapter discusses how deficiencies in nutrients such as vitamin D, B vitamins, and magnesium can affect mood and anxiety-related symptoms. Adequate intake of these micronutrients is crucial for maintaining emotional well-being.

Inflammation and Antioxidants

The chapter delves into the connection between inflammation and anxiety. Chronic low-grade inflammation, often associated with genetic predisposition, can exacerbate anxiety symptoms. Antioxidants found in fruits, vegetables, and other nutrient-rich foods are explored for their potential to counteract inflammation and oxidative stress.

Probiotics and Gut Health

Probiotics are discussed as agents that can influence the gut microbiome and promote gut health. Emerging research suggests that probiotics might have a modulating effect on anxiety-related neural circuits, potentially mitigating the impact of genetic predisposition.

Sugar and Caffeine

The chapter discusses the impact of sugar and caffeine on anxiety. Excessive sugar intake and high caffeine consumption can lead to energy fluctuations, disrupted sleep, and increased physiological arousal, exacerbating genetic anxiety responses.

Balanced Diet and Mood Stabilization

The importance of a balanced diet in stabilizing mood and reducing anxiety is underscored. A diet rich in whole grains, lean proteins, healthy fats, and a variety of fruits and vegetables provides the nutrients needed for emotional well-being.

Mindful Eating and Emotional Regulation

The chapter explores mindful eating as a strategy to enhance emotional regulation. Mindful eating involves paying attention to the sensory experience of eating, which can foster a healthier relationship with food and prevent emotional eating triggered by genetic anxiety.

Personalized Nutrition and Genetic Variations

The integration of personalized nutrition with genetic variations is discussed. Nutrigenomics, the study of how genes interact with nutrients, is explored as a potential avenue to tailor dietary recommendations based on an individual's genetic predisposition to anxiety.

Conclusion

"The Role of Nutrition in Alleviating Genetic Anxiety" concludes by highlighting the transformative potential of dietary choices in managing genetic anxiety. The chapter underscores that by selecting nutrient-dense foods that support brain health and emotional well-being, individuals can mitigate the impact of genetic predisposition on anxiety-related symptoms, ultimately fostering a state of balance and resilience.

CHAPTER 14: EXERCISE AS A NATURAL ANTIDOTE TO GENETIC ANXIETY

Introduction

Exercise emerges as a natural antidote to genetic anxiety, offering a holistic approach that positively influences neurotransmitter balance, stress response, and overall emotional well-being. Chapter 14, titled "Exercise as a Natural Antidote to Genetic Anxiety," delves into the transformative potential of physical activity in alleviating the impact of genetic predisposition on anxiety-related symptoms.

Understanding the Connection: Exercise and Anxiety

The chapter begins by introducing the connection between exercise and anxiety. It highlights how physical activity can modulate neural pathways, release mood-enhancing neurotransmitters, and promote neuroplastic changes that counteract the genetic influence on anxiety.

Neurotransmitter Release and Mood Regulation

Exploring the role of exercise in neurotransmitter release, the chapter discusses how physical activity can stimulate the production of endorphins, dopamine, and serotonin - neurotransmitters that contribute to mood regulation, stress reduction, and emotional well-being.

Stress Response Modulation

The impact of exercise on stress response modulation is highlighted. Regular physical activity can enhance the body's ability to cope with stressors, reducing the physiological and psychological impact of genetic predisposition on anxiety.

Neuroplasticity and Cognitive Resilience

The chapter delves into how exercise can promote neuroplasticity, the brain's ability to rewire and adapt. Neuroplastic changes induced by physical activity can counteract the genetic tendency toward heightened anxiety responses, enhancing cognitive resilience.

Aerobic vs. Anaerobic Exercise

The distinction between aerobic and anaerobic exercise is discussed. Aerobic activities like jogging and swimming are highlighted for their capacity to enhance cardiovascular fitness and promote the release of mood-enhancing neurotransmitters.

Mind-Body Activities: Yoga and Tai Chi

Mind-body activities such as yoga and tai chi are explored as forms of exercise that integrate movement with mindfulness and relaxation techniques. These practices can foster emotional regulation, reduce muscle tension, and counteract the physiological effects of genetic anxiety.

Frequency, Duration, and Intensity

The chapter discusses the optimal frequency, duration, and intensity of exercise for managing genetic anxiety. It emphasizes that consistency in physical activity is key, and individuals should aim for a balance that aligns with their fitness level and lifestyle.

Social Interaction and Support

The social aspect of exercise is highlighted. Engaging in group activities, sports, or fitness classes can foster a sense of belonging, reduce isolation, and counteract the genetic tendency toward social anxiety.

Outdoor Activities and Nature

The connection between outdoor activities and anxiety relief is explored. Spending time in nature can provide a sense of calm, reduce rumination, and complement the stress-reducing effects of exercise.

Incorporating Exercise Into Daily Life

The chapter discusses strategies for incorporating exercise into daily life. It emphasizes that individuals can find opportunities for physical activity throughout their routines, whether it's through walking, cycling, or taking the stairs.

Long-Term Benefits and Resilience

The chapter underscores the long-term benefits of exercise in building resilience against genetic predisposition. Regular physical activity can lead to lasting changes in neural circuits, neurotransmitter balance, and stress response, ultimately countering the impact of genetic anxiety over time.

Conclusion

"Exercise as a Natural Antidote to Genetic Anxiety" concludes by highlighting the transformative potential of physical activity in managing genetic anxiety. The chapter underscores that exercise offers a powerful means to recalibrate the nervous system, promote emotional well-being, and mitigate the impact of genetic predisposition on anxiety-related symptoms, ultimately fostering a state of balance, strength, and resilience.

CHAPTER 15: MEDICATION OPTIONS FOR GENETIC ANXIETY: BALANCING RISKS AND BENEFITS

Introduction

Medication options play a significant role in managing genetic anxiety, offering a pharmacological approach that aims to balance the risks and benefits of intervention. Chapter 15, titled "Medication Options for Genetic Anxiety: Balancing Risks and Benefits," delves into the diverse array of medications available for alleviating the impact of genetic predisposition on anxiety-related symptoms, while addressing the complexities of individual response and potential side effects.

Understanding Medication for Anxiety

The chapter begins by introducing the concept of medication as a tool for managing genetic anxiety. It emphasizes that medication is often considered when anxiety symptoms significantly interfere with an individual's quality of life.

Selective Serotonin Reuptake Inhibitors (SSRIs)

Exploring medication options, SSRIs are highlighted as a commonly prescribed class of antidepressants used for anxiety disorders. The chapter discusses how SSRIs work by increasing serotonin levels in the brain, promoting mood stability and reducing the physiological effects of genetic anxiety.

Serotonin-Norepinephrine Reuptake Inhibitors (SNRIs)

The role of SNRIs is explored as an alternative class of antidepressants that target both serotonin and norepinephrine. SNRIs are discussed for their potential to address a broader range of anxiety symptoms and provide relief from genetic anxiety-related distress.

Benzodiazepines

The chapter delves into benzodiazepines, a class of medications that exert sedative and anxiolytic effects. While effective in rapidly reducing anxiety symptoms, the potential for dependence and withdrawal is discussed, highlighting the need for cautious use and short-term treatment.

Beta-Blockers

The role of beta-blockers in managing the physiological symptoms of anxiety is explored. These medications can alleviate symptoms such as rapid heart rate and trembling, offering relief from the genetic predisposition to heightened stress responses.

Atypical Antipsychotics

The chapter discusses the use of atypical antipsychotics as augmentation strategies for treatment-resistant anxiety disorders. These medications are explored for their potential to modulate neurotransmitter activity and target severe symptoms associated with genetic anxiety.

Antihistamines and Antidepressants

Certain antihistamines and tricyclic antidepressants are explored for their off-label use in managing anxiety symptoms. The chapter discusses how these medications can influence neurotransmitter systems, offering an alternative pharmacological approach.

Personalized Medication Management

The importance of personalized medication management is emphasized. Individuals respond differently to medications due to genetic variations, and finding the right medication, dosage, and combination requires a collaborative approach between patients and healthcare providers.

Balancing Risks and Benefits

The chapter discusses the importance of balancing the risks

and benefits of medication. Potential side effects, interactions, and individual response are explored, emphasizing the need for informed decision-making and ongoing monitoring.

Medication Combined with Other Strategies

The chapter underscores that medication is often most effective when combined with other strategies, such as therapy, lifestyle modifications, and coping techniques. The comprehensive approach aims to address genetic predisposition within a holistic context.

Tapering and Discontinuation

The chapter concludes by discussing the importance of tapering and discontinuing medications under medical supervision. Gradual tapering minimizes withdrawal symptoms and allows for the assessment of how well other strategies are managing genetic anxiety.

Conclusion

"Medication Options for Genetic Anxiety: Balancing Risks and Benefits" concludes by highlighting the complexities of medication management in the context of genetic anxiety. The chapter underscores that while medication can offer relief, it is just one facet of a multifaceted approach that addresses the intricate interplay of genetics, psychology, and environment. By navigating the nuances of medication use, individuals can find a balance that enhances their ability to manage genetic anxiety while minimizing potential risks.

CHAPTER 16: EXPLORING ALTERNATIVE THERAPIES: FROM ACUPUNCTURE TO YOGA

Introduction

Beyond conventional approaches, alternative therapies provide a diverse range of strategies for managing genetic anxiety, emphasizing holistic well-being and individual empowerment. Chapter 16, titled "Exploring Alternative Therapies: From Acupuncture to Yoga," delves into the world of non-traditional therapeutic modalities that can offer unique perspectives and tools for alleviating the impact of genetic predisposition on anxiety-related symptoms.

Understanding Alternative Therapies

The chapter begins by introducing alternative therapies and their focus on addressing the mind-body connection. It highlights the shift towards a more integrative and holistic approach to mental health, acknowledging the importance of individualized care.

Acupuncture and Traditional Chinese Medicine

Exploring acupuncture, the chapter discusses how this ancient practice from Traditional Chinese Medicine involves stimulating specific points on the body to promote energy flow and balance. Acupuncture is explored for its potential to alleviate anxiety-related symptoms and counteract the genetic influence on stress responses.

Herbal Remedies and Supplements

The role of herbal remedies and supplements is discussed in the context of anxiety management. Adaptogens, herbs, and natural compounds such as ashwagandha, valerian root, and CBD are explored for their potential to modulate stress response and provide relief from genetic anxiety.

Aromatherapy and Essential Oils

The chapter delves into aromatherapy and essential oils as tools for emotional regulation. Certain scents like lavender and chamomile are explored for their potential to calm the nervous system and promote relaxation, offering a sensory-based approach to managing genetic predisposition.

Massage Therapy and Bodywork

The impact of massage therapy and bodywork on anxiety relief is highlighted. These practices can reduce muscle tension, enhance circulation, and induce a sense of relaxation that counteracts the physiological effects of genetic predisposition.

Mind-Body Practices: Yoga and Tai Chi

Mind-body practices such as yoga and tai chi are explored in greater depth. These practices combine movement, breathwork, and mindfulness to enhance emotional regulation, reduce stress, and counteract the genetic predisposition to heightened anxiety.

Meditation and Mindfulness-Based Therapies

The chapter discusses meditation and mindfulness-based therapies beyond the introductory context. Mindfulness-Based Stress Reduction (MBSR) and Mindfulness-Based Cognitive Therapy (MBCT) are explored as structured programs that promote emotional well-being and resilience against genetic anxiety.

Biofeedback and Neurofeedback

The role of biofeedback and neurofeedback is highlighted. These techniques involve monitoring physiological responses and providing real-time feedback, helping individuals regulate stress responses and mitigate the physiological effects of genetic anxiety.

Energy Healing and Reiki

Exploring energy healing practices like Reiki, the chapter discusses how these therapies focus on balancing energy flow within the body. Reiki is explored for its potential to promote relaxation, reduce tension, and alleviate the impact of genetic predisposition on anxiety.

Art Therapy and Creative Expression

The chapter delves into art therapy and creative expression as tools for emotional catharsis. Engaging in artistic activities can provide a means to process emotions, reduce rumination, and counteract the psychological impact of genetic anxiety.

Conclusion

"Exploring Alternative Therapies: From Acupuncture to Yoga" concludes by emphasizing the richness and diversity of alternative therapies available for managing genetic anxiety. The chapter underscores that these therapies offer individualized and holistic approaches that can complement conventional strategies. By exploring alternative pathways, individuals can discover tools that resonate with their unique needs, ultimately enhancing their ability to navigate the complexities of genetic predisposition and anxiety-related symptoms.

CHAPTER 17: NURTURING EMOTIONAL WELL-BEING IN THE FACE OF GENETIC ANXIETY

Introduction

Nurturing emotional well-being becomes paramount when facing genetic anxiety, as it involves cultivating resilience, fostering self-compassion, and embracing a positive outlook on life. Chapter 17, titled "Nurturing Emotional Well-being in the Face of Genetic Anxiety," delves into the profound journey of emotional growth and self-care that empowers individuals to thrive despite the challenges posed by genetic predisposition.

Understanding Emotional Well-being

The chapter begins by introducing the concept of emotional well-being and its significance in managing genetic anxiety. It underscores the importance of building a foundation of emotional strength and resilience.

Self-Compassion and Acceptance

Exploring self-compassion, the chapter discusses how individuals can cultivate kindness toward themselves, counteracting self-criticism often exacerbated by genetic predisposition. Self-acceptance is explored as a fundamental aspect of nurturing emotional well-being.

Positive Psychology and Gratitude

The role of positive psychology and gratitude is highlighted. The chapter delves into how focusing on strengths, cultivating optimism, and practicing gratitude can shift one's perspective and counteract the genetic inclination toward negative thought patterns.

Emotional Intelligence and Self-Awareness

Exploring emotional intelligence, the chapter discusses how enhancing self-awareness and understanding emotions can promote effective coping. Emotional intelligence can empower individuals to navigate genetic anxiety with greater resilience and adaptability.

Stress Reduction and Relaxation Techniques

The impact of stress reduction and relaxation techniques on emotional well-being is explored. These practices, including mindfulness, meditation, and deep breathing, can foster emotional regulation and mitigate the physiological effects of genetic predisposition.

Mindful Self-Compassion

The integration of mindfulness and self-compassion is discussed. Mindful self-compassion involves applying mindfulness principles to self-critical thoughts, fostering a gentle and understanding attitude toward oneself that counters the genetic predisposition to heightened self-judgment.

Cultivating Positive Relationships

The chapter delves into the role of positive relationships in emotional well-being. Building strong connections with supportive individuals can provide validation, understanding, and a sense of belonging that counteracts the isolating effects of genetic anxiety.

Cognitive Resilience and Reframing

Cognitive resilience through cognitive-behavioral techniques is explored. By challenging negative thought patterns and reframing perceptions, individuals can mitigate the psychological impact of genetic predisposition and foster a more optimistic outlook.

Creating a Wellness Routine

The chapter discusses the creation of a personalized wellness routine that integrates various strategies for emotional well-being. This routine can encompass mindfulness practices, exercise, social engagement, creative outlets, and other tools that resonate with individual preferences.

Professional Support and Therapy

The importance of seeking professional support is underscored. Therapists can provide guidance, insight, and evidence-based interventions that address the emotional complexities of genetic anxiety.

Long-Term Emotional Growth

The chapter concludes by emphasizing that nurturing emotional well-being is a journey of growth and self-discovery. It underscores that emotional well-being is not a destination but a continuous process of building resilience, adapting to challenges, and embracing life's fluctuations with grace and strength.

Conclusion

"Nurturing Emotional Well-being in the Face of Genetic Anxiety" concludes by highlighting the transformative potential of fostering emotional strength and resilience. The chapter underscores that while genetic predisposition may set the stage, emotional well-being empowers individuals to rewrite their stories, redefine their relationships with anxiety, and cultivate a sense of purpose and contentment in the face of adversity.

CHAPTER 18: BUILDING STRONG SOCIAL SUPPORT SYSTEMS FOR GENETIC ANXIETY

Introduction

Building robust social support systems becomes essential in the context of genetic anxiety, as meaningful connections and empathetic relationships can counteract the isolating effects of anxiety-related symptoms. Chapter 18, titled "Building Strong Social Support Systems for Genetic Anxiety," delves into the intricate web of relationships that individuals can cultivate to enhance their resilience, foster understanding, and alleviate the impact of genetic predisposition on anxiety.

Understanding the Role of Social Support

The chapter begins by introducing the role of social support in managing genetic anxiety. It highlights how social connections provide a buffer against the psychological and physiological effects of anxiety-related symptoms.

Family Support and Understanding

Exploring family support, the chapter discusses the importance of open communication and understanding within familial relationships. Families can offer validation, empathy, and a sense of safety that counteracts the genetic predisposition to isolation.

Friendships and Peer Relationships

The impact of friendships and peer relationships on anxiety management is explored. Friends can provide companionship, distraction, and opportunities for social engagement that reduce the impact of genetic anxiety on emotional well-being.

Support Groups and Community Engagement

The chapter delves into the role of support groups and community engagement. Joining groups that share similar experiences can offer a sense of belonging, normalize feelings, and provide practical coping strategies for genetic anxiety.

Partner Support and Intimate Relationships

The importance of partner support in intimate relationships is highlighted. Partners can offer understanding, emotional validation, and a safe space for vulnerability that counteracts the genetic predisposition to heightened anxiety responses.

Professional Support and Therapeutic Relationships

Exploring professional support, the chapter discusses the therapeutic relationships individuals can cultivate with mental health professionals. Therapists offer guidance, coping strategies, and evidence-based interventions that address the psychological complexities of genetic anxiety.

Empathy and Active Listening

The chapter emphasizes the role of empathy and active listening in social support. Being present, showing empathy, and offering a nonjudgmental space can alleviate feelings of isolation and enhance emotional well-being.

Online Support and Virtual Communities

The impact of online support groups and virtual communities is explored. The digital landscape offers platforms for individuals to connect, share experiences, and receive support, even when physical interactions are limited.

Boundaries and Self-Care in Relationships

The chapter discusses the importance of setting boundaries and practicing self-care within relationships. Individuals with genetic anxiety must prioritize their well-being and communicate their needs to ensure that social support remains beneficial.

Cultivating Reciprocity in Relationships

The chapter underscores the importance of reciprocity in relationships. Fostering a balanced give-and-take dynamic ensures that individuals with genetic anxiety both receive and contribute support within their social networks.

Long-Term Relationship Building

The chapter concludes by emphasizing that building strong social support systems is a long-term endeavor. It underscores those nurturing relationships involves continuous effort, communication, and a willingness to adapt and grow together.

Conclusion

"Building Strong Social Support Systems for Genetic Anxiety" concludes by highlighting the transformative power of meaningful connections. The chapter underscores that while genetic predisposition may shape the landscape of anxiety, social support systems provide a foundation of understanding, validation, and shared strength that empowers individuals to face the challenges of genetic anxiety with resilience, authenticity, and a sense of belonging.

CHAPTER 19: GENETIC ANXIETY IN CHILDREN: EARLY INTERVENTION AND SUPPORT

Introduction

Genetic anxiety in children necessitates early intervention and targeted support to promote healthy emotional development and prevent long-term impact. Chapter 19, titled "Genetic Anxiety in Children: Early Intervention and Support," delves into the unique challenges of identifying, understanding, and addressing anxiety-related symptoms in children with a genetic predisposition, emphasizing the importance of nurturing their emotional well-being from an early age.

Understanding Genetic Anxiety in Children

The chapter begins by introducing the concept of genetic anxiety in children. It underscores that genetics can play a role in shaping anxiety responses and behaviors from a young age.

Early Signs and Identification

Exploring the early signs of genetic anxiety, the chapter discusses how children may exhibit symptoms such as excessive worry, avoidance, physical complaints, and changes in behavior. Identifying these signs early allows for timely intervention.

The Role of Genetics in Childhood Anxiety

The chapter delves into the role of genetics in childhood anxiety. It highlights how genetic predisposition interacts with environmental factors to shape a child's anxiety responses and vulnerability.

Parental Modeling and Anxiety Transmission

The impact of parental modeling on anxiety transmission to

children is explored. Parents' own experiences with anxiety can influence children's perceptions and coping mechanisms, underscoring the importance of parental awareness and modeling healthy behaviors.

Early Intervention Strategies

The chapter discusses early intervention strategies for genetic anxiety in children. These strategies include psychoeducation, teaching coping skills, encouraging open communication, and promoting emotional regulation through creative outlets.

School-Based Support

Exploring school-based support, the chapter discusses how educators can play a crucial role in identifying and supporting children with genetic anxiety. Creating a nurturing and inclusive classroom environment is essential for children's emotional well-being.

Play Therapy and Creative Expression

The impact of play therapy and creative expression in children's anxiety management is highlighted. Play-based interventions offer a safe space for children to explore emotions, build resilience, and process their experiences.

Parental Guidance and Support

The chapter emphasizes the importance of parental guidance and support. Parents can provide comfort, reassurance, and understanding that counteracts the genetic predisposition to heightened anxiety responses.

Professional Assessment and Treatment

Exploring professional assessment and treatment, the chapter discusses the role of mental health professionals in working with children with genetic anxiety. Child psychologists and therapists offer evidence-based interventions tailored to children's developmental needs.

Fostering Resilience and Emotional Regulation

The chapter delves into the importance of fostering resilience and emotional regulation in children. By equipping children with coping skills, problem-solving techniques, and a strong emotional foundation, parents and caregivers can mitigate the impact of genetic predisposition on anxiety-related symptoms.

Parent-Child Communication and Attachment

The role of parent-child communication and attachment in managing genetic anxiety is explored. Open dialogues and secure attachments offer children a safe haven to express their feelings and seek comfort.

Long-Term Emotional Well-being

The chapter concludes by emphasizing that early intervention and support lay the groundwork for children's long-term emotional well-being. It underscores that by providing tools, understanding, and a nurturing environment, children can learn to navigate the complexities of genetic anxiety with resilience, self-awareness, and a sense of agency.

Conclusion

"Genetic Anxiety in Children: Early Intervention and Support" concludes by highlighting the transformative potential of early intervention in shaping children's emotional trajectories. The chapter underscores that by addressing genetic anxiety in its early stages, children can develop the skills, confidence, and emotional well-being to thrive despite genetic predisposition, ultimately paving the way for a future marked by strength, adaptability, and resilience.

CHAPTER 20: ADOLESCENTS AND GENETIC ANXIETY: GUIDING RESILIENCE AND GROWTH

Introduction

Adolescence is a critical period for addressing genetic anxiety, as young individuals navigate identity development, peer interactions, and increased stressors. Chapter 20, titled "Adolescents and Genetic Anxiety: Guiding Resilience and Growth," delves into the complexities of managing anxiety-related symptoms in adolescents with a genetic predisposition, emphasizing the role of guidance, empowerment, and fostering emotional resilience during this transformative life stage.

Understanding Genetic Anxiety in Adolescents

The chapter begins by introducing the unique challenges of genetic anxiety in adolescents. It highlights how genetic predisposition interacts with developmental changes to shape adolescents' experiences of anxiety.

Identity Development and Anxiety

Exploring identity development, the chapter discusses how adolescents' search for identity can intersect with anxiety-related symptoms. Genetic predisposition may influence the ways in which adolescents perceive and cope with identity-related stressors.

Peer Relationships and Social Anxiety

The impact of peer relationships on anxiety, particularly social anxiety, is explored. Adolescents with a genetic predisposition may experience heightened sensitivity to peer interactions, highlighting the importance of building supportive social networks.

Academic Pressure and Performance Anxiety

The chapter delves into academic pressure and performance anxiety. Adolescents may grapple with genetic predisposition amplifying the stress of academic expectations, necessitating strategies to manage perfectionism and promote a healthy approach to achievement.

Navigating Digital Stressors

Exploring digital stressors, the chapter discusses how technology and social media can exacerbate anxiety symptoms in adolescents. Genetic predisposition may influence how adolescents perceive and respond to online interactions and pressures.

Communication and Parental Involvement

The chapter emphasizes the role of communication and parental involvement in managing genetic anxiety during adolescence. Open dialogues, active listening, and collaboration empower adolescents to seek guidance and support.

Building Coping Skills and Emotional Regulation

The importance of building coping skills and emotional regulation is highlighted. Adolescents can learn strategies to manage stress, develop resilience, and counteract the physiological effects of genetic predisposition.

Peer Support and Group Therapy

Exploring peer support and group therapy, the chapter discusses how adolescents can benefit from connecting with peers who share similar experiences. Group settings provide validation, understanding, and shared coping strategies.

Cognitive-Behavioral Techniques for Adolescents

The chapter delves into cognitive-behavioral techniques tailored to adolescents. Techniques such as cognitive restructuring, exposure therapy, and mindfulness can empower adolescents to challenge negative thought patterns and manage genetic anxiety.

Future Orientation and Goal Setting

The impact of future orientation and goal setting on anxiety management is explored. Adolescents with genetic anxiety can benefit from setting achievable goals, fostering a sense of purpose, and focusing on positive future outcomes.

Transition to Adulthood and Resilience

The chapter discusses the transition to adulthood and the cultivation of resilience. Adolescents can develop skills to adapt to life changes, make informed decisions, and navigate the challenges of genetic predisposition.

Promoting Self-Care and Well-being

The chapter concludes by emphasizing the importance of promoting self-care and well-being in adolescents. It underscores that by equipping adolescents with self-care strategies, self-awareness, and emotional intelligence, parents, caregivers, and professionals can guide them toward a path of growth, resilience, and emotional strength.

Conclusion

"Adolescents and Genetic Anxiety: Guiding Resilience and Growth" concludes by highlighting the transformative potential of guiding adolescents through the challenges of genetic anxiety. The chapter underscores that by providing understanding, mentorship, and empowerment, adolescents can harness their innate capacity for growth, navigate genetic predisposition with strength, and embark on a journey toward adulthood marked by resilience, self-acceptance, and the skills to thrive despite anxiety-related challenges.

CHAPTER 21: ADULTING WITH GENETIC ANXIETY: STRATEGIES FOR SUCCESS

Introduction

Navigating adulthood while dealing with genetic anxiety presents unique challenges, as individuals face increasing responsibilities, career pressures, and personal relationships. Chapter 21, titled "Adulting with Genetic Anxiety: Strategies for Success," delves into the complexities of managing anxiety-related symptoms in adults with a genetic predisposition, emphasizing the development of effective coping strategies, self-care practices, and resilience-building techniques to thrive in various aspects of adult life.

Understanding Genetic Anxiety in Adults

The chapter begins by introducing the realities of genetic anxiety in adulthood. It underscores how genetic predisposition intersects with the demands of adulthood, shaping individuals' experiences of anxiety and influencing their coping mechanisms.

Career Development and Workplace Anxiety

Exploring career development and workplace anxiety, the chapter discusses how genetic predisposition may influence how individuals navigate job-related stressors. Strategies for managing performance anxiety, imposter syndrome, and work-life balance are explored.

Financial Stress and Anxiety

The impact of financial stress on anxiety is discussed. Genetic predisposition may contribute to heightened financial anxiety, highlighting the importance of financial planning, budgeting, and seeking professional guidance.

Relationships and Intimacy

The chapter delves into the role of relationships and intimacy in managing genetic anxiety. Building healthy communication skills, addressing attachment-related concerns, and fostering emotional intimacy are explored.

Parenting and Balancing Responsibilities

Exploring parenting and the balancing of responsibilities, the chapter discusses how individuals with genetic anxiety can manage the challenges of raising children while dealing with their own anxiety-related symptoms. Effective parenting strategies, self-care, and seeking support are highlighted.

Time Management and Stress Reduction

The importance of time management and stress reduction is emphasized. Effective time management techniques can alleviate the pressures of adult life, while stress reduction practices counteract the physiological effects of genetic predisposition.

Effective Communication and Boundaries

The chapter discusses effective communication and boundary-setting in adult relationships. Individuals with genetic anxiety can benefit from assertive communication and clear boundaries that foster understanding and emotional well-being.

Professional Growth and Lifelong Learning

Exploring professional growth and lifelong learning, the chapter highlights how adults with genetic anxiety can focus on personal development, skill enhancement, and continuous learning to counteract stagnation and anxiety-related concerns.

Therapeutic Approaches and Self-Reflection

The chapter delves into therapeutic approaches for adults with genetic anxiety. Individual therapy, group therapy, and self-reflection practices can offer insights, coping strategies, and emotional regulation techniques.

Mindfulness and Resilience

The impact of mindfulness and resilience-building on anxiety management is explored. Mindfulness practices enhance present-moment awareness, while resilience-building techniques foster adaptability and emotional strength.

Cultivating Joy and Meaning

The chapter emphasizes the importance of cultivating joy and meaning in adulthood. Engaging in hobbies, pursuing passions, and fostering a sense of purpose counteract the genetic predisposition to rumination and negative thought patterns.

Personal Growth and Long-Term Well-being

The chapter concludes by highlighting the transformative potential of personal growth and well-being in adulthood. It underscores that by embracing strategies for success, individuals can navigate the complexities of genetic anxiety with resilience, adaptability, and a commitment to a fulfilling adult life.

Conclusion

"Adulting with Genetic Anxiety: Strategies for Success" concludes by highlighting the power of intentional choices and strategies in adult life. The chapter underscores that while genetic predisposition may shape the landscape of anxiety, adults can develop the skills, perspectives, and emotional well-being to thrive despite the challenges, ultimately paving the way for a life marked by growth, self-empowerment, and the ability to overcome anxiety-related obstacles.

CHAPTER 22: NAVIGATING RELATIONSHIPS WHEN GENETIC ANXIETY IS AT PLAY

Introduction

Genetic anxiety can profoundly impact relationships, affecting communication, intimacy, and emotional dynamics. Chapter 22, titled "Navigating Relationships When Genetic Anxiety Is at Play," delves into the intricacies of managing relationships when one or both individuals experience anxiety-related symptoms due to genetic predisposition. This chapter explores strategies for fostering understanding, promoting empathy, and building strong connections despite the challenges posed by anxiety.

Understanding the Impact on Relationships

The chapter begins by introducing the impact of genetic anxiety on relationships. It highlights how anxiety-related symptoms can influence communication patterns, conflict resolution, and emotional intimacy.

Open Communication and Shared Understanding

Exploring open communication, the chapter discusses the importance of sharing feelings and concerns related to genetic anxiety. Partners can develop a shared understanding that counteracts misunderstandings and cultivates empathy.

Empathy and Validation

The role of empathy and validation in relationships is emphasized. Partners can provide emotional support, validation, and a safe space for expressing anxiety-related experiences.

Supportive Listening and Active Engagement

Exploring supportive listening, the chapter discusses how active engagement can enhance emotional intimacy. Partners who listen attentively, offer validation, and refrain from judgment create an environment that fosters connection.

Navigating Triggers and Sensitivities

The chapter delves into the navigation of triggers and sensitivities related to genetic anxiety. Partners can learn to recognize anxiety-related cues and respond with compassion and sensitivity.

Couples Therapy and Relationship Enhancement

Exploring couples therapy, the chapter discusses how therapy can provide a structured setting for addressing anxiety-related challenges. Relationship enhancement techniques can foster understanding, effective communication, and conflict resolution.

Setting Boundaries and Self-Care

The importance of setting boundaries and practicing self-care within relationships is highlighted. Individuals with genetic anxiety can communicate their needs while supporting their partners in understanding these boundaries.

Partner Involvement in Coping Strategies

The chapter emphasizes the role of partners in coping strategies. Partners can engage in relaxation techniques, participate in activities that alleviate anxiety, and learn to support each other's well-being.

Empowerment and Personal Growth

Exploring empowerment and personal growth within relationships, the chapter discusses how partners can encourage each other's journeys toward managing genetic anxiety. Mutual support enhances personal growth and resilience.

Building Shared Coping Strategies

The chapter delves into the creation of shared coping strategies.

Partners can collaboratively develop techniques that alleviate anxiety-related symptoms and strengthen their bond.

Promoting Trust and Security

The importance of promoting trust and security in relationships is explored. Partners can foster trust by consistently demonstrating empathy, reliability, and emotional availability.

Long-Term Relationship Sustainability

The chapter concludes by emphasizing the sustainability of relationships when managing genetic anxiety. It underscores that by embracing strategies that foster empathy, open communication, and mutual growth, partners can navigate the complexities of anxiety-related challenges, ultimately creating a relationship marked by strength, resilience, and shared emotional well-being.

Conclusion

"Navigating Relationships When Genetic Anxiety Is at Play" concludes by highlighting the transformative power of relationships built on understanding and empathy. The chapter underscores that while genetic predisposition may influence anxiety, partners can create a space that nurtures each other's emotional well-being, promotes resilience, and empowers both individuals to thrive despite the challenges posed by anxiety-related symptoms.

CHAPTER 23: PARENTING THROUGH GENETIC ANXIETY: LESSONS AND INSIGHTS

Introduction

Parenting through the lens of genetic anxiety requires sensitivity, understanding, and effective strategies to support children who may inherit anxiety-related traits. Chapter 23, titled "Parenting Through Genetic Anxiety: Lessons and Insights," delves into the challenges and opportunities that arise when parents navigate the complexities of genetic anxiety within their families. This chapter explores valuable insights, parenting approaches, and tools for nurturing emotional well-being in children who may be genetically predisposed to anxiety.

Understanding Genetic Anxiety in Parenting

The chapter begins by introducing the concept of genetic anxiety in the context of parenting. It underscores how genetic predisposition can influence children's anxiety responses and shape parenting experiences.

Modeling Healthy Coping

Exploring modeling healthy coping, the chapter discusses how parents' own approaches to anxiety management can impact their children's perceptions and behaviors. Parents can model healthy coping strategies and emotional regulation.

Creating a Supportive Environment

The importance of creating a supportive environment is emphasized. Parents can foster open communication, validation, and a safe space where children feel comfortable discussing their anxiety-related experiences.

Educational Awareness and Psychoeducation

Exploring educational awareness, the chapter discusses how parents can educate themselves about anxiety and its genetic components. Psychoeducation equips parents with knowledge to address children's questions and concerns.

Validating Children's Emotions

The chapter delves into the significance of validating children's emotions. Parents can offer validation, empathy, and reassurance that counteract the genetic predisposition to heightened anxiety responses.

Teaching Coping Skills

The role of teaching coping skills is highlighted. Parents can equip children with age-appropriate coping strategies that promote emotional resilience and self-regulation.

Promoting Emotional Intelligence

Exploring emotional intelligence, the chapter discusses how parents can foster emotional awareness and understanding in children. Emotional intelligence equips children to navigate anxiety-related emotions effectively.

Encouraging Open Dialogue

The importance of encouraging open dialogue about anxiety is explored. Parents can create an environment where children feel comfortable discussing their feelings, fears, and questions.

Building Resilience and Self-Esteem

The chapter emphasizes building resilience and self-esteem in children. Parents can promote a growth mindset, encourage problem-solving, and celebrate children's achievements to counteract the genetic predisposition to self-doubt.

Avoiding Overprotection

Exploring avoiding overprotection, the chapter discusses how parents can strike a balance between offering support and allowing children to face challenges. Avoiding overprotection fosters independence and self-confidence.

Seeking Professional Guidance

The chapter discusses the role of seeking professional guidance when parenting through genetic anxiety. Mental health professionals can offer insights, interventions, and support tailored to children's developmental needs.

Cultivating a Nonjudgmental Atmosphere

The chapter delves into cultivating a nonjudgmental atmosphere. Parents can convey unconditional love, acceptance, and a nonjudgmental stance that promotes emotional security.

Long-Term Parenting Reflection

The chapter concludes by emphasizing the importance of long-term parenting reflection. Parenting through genetic anxiety is an ongoing journey of learning, adapting, and nurturing children's emotional well-being.

Conclusion

"Parenting Through Genetic Anxiety: Lessons and Insights" concludes by highlighting the transformative power of parenting that acknowledges and addresses genetic anxiety. The chapter underscores that while genetics may influence the landscape of anxiety, parents can provide a foundation of understanding, support, and emotional tools that empower children to navigate their anxiety-related challenges with resilience, self-compassion, and the ability to thrive despite their genetic predisposition.

CHAPTER 24: THRIVING IN THE WORKPLACE DESPITE GENETIC ANXIETY

Introduction

Thriving in the workplace while managing genetic anxiety requires a combination of self-awareness, effective coping strategies, and a supportive work environment. Chapter 24, titled "Thriving in the Workplace Despite Genetic Anxiety," delves into the intricacies of navigating the demands of a professional setting while dealing with anxiety-related symptoms influenced by genetic predisposition. This chapter explores strategies for optimizing performance, fostering well-being, and achieving success in one's career.

Understanding the Intersection of Genetic Anxiety and the Workplace

The chapter begins by introducing the intersection of genetic anxiety and the workplace. It highlights how genetic predisposition can influence individuals' experiences of workplace stressors and anxiety-related responses.

Self-Awareness and Identifying Triggers

Exploring self-awareness, the chapter discusses the importance of identifying anxiety triggers within the workplace. Recognizing specific situations or contexts that amplify anxiety-related symptoms enables individuals to develop targeted coping strategies.

Effective Time Management

The impact of effective time management on anxiety management is explored. Planning, prioritizing tasks, and setting realistic goals can alleviate the pressure of workplace demands and counteract the physiological effects of genetic predisposition.

Stress Reduction Techniques

The chapter delves into stress reduction techniques that can be applied in the workplace. Mindfulness, deep breathing, and short breaks can promote emotional regulation and enhance resilience against genetic anxiety.

Healthy Work-Life Boundaries

Exploring healthy work-life boundaries, the chapter discusses how individuals can set limits to prevent work-related stress from permeating their personal lives. Establishing boundaries fosters a sense of control and emotional well-being.

Effective Communication and Advocacy

The role of effective communication and self-advocacy in the workplace is emphasized. Openly discussing one's anxiety-related needs with supervisors and colleagues can lead to tailored support and accommodations.

Cultivating Supportive Work Relationships

Exploring cultivating supportive work relationships, the chapter discusses how individuals can foster connections that alleviate feelings of isolation. Building relationships with colleagues who offer understanding and empathy can create a supportive work environment.

Mindful Career Choices

The chapter highlights the significance of mindful career choices. Individuals can align their career paths with their strengths, values, and interests to reduce work-related stress and enhance job satisfaction.

Professional Development and Skill Enhancement

Exploring professional development, the chapter discusses how individuals can focus on skill enhancement and continuous learning. Gaining expertise in one's field promotes confidence and counteracts anxiety-related self-doubt.

Utilizing EAPs and Workplace Resources

The chapter discusses the utilization of Employee Assistance Programs (EAPs) and workplace resources. These programs offer counseling, support, and resources that can enhance emotional well-being in the face of genetic anxiety.

Promoting a Positive Work Culture

The impact of promoting a positive work culture on anxiety management is explored. Employers and employees can contribute to a supportive atmosphere that values mental health, well-being, and mutual respect.

Long-Term Career Growth and Fulfillment

The chapter concludes by emphasizing the potential for long-term career growth and fulfillment despite genetic anxiety. It underscores that while genetics may influence anxiety responses, individuals can employ strategies that enhance their professional journey, promote resilience, and lead to a fulfilling and successful career.

Conclusion

"Thriving in the Workplace Despite Genetic Anxiety" concludes by highlighting the transformative power of strategies for success in the professional realm. The chapter underscores that while genetic predisposition may shape the landscape of anxiety, individuals can develop the skills, self-awareness, and emotional well-being to excel in their careers, ultimately paving the way for a future marked by growth, achievement, and the ability to thrive despite anxiety-related challenges.

CHAPTER 25: GENETIC ANXIETY AND ITS IMPACT ON ROMANTIC RELATIONSHIPS

Introduction

Genetic anxiety can significantly influence romantic relationships, shaping communication, intimacy, and overall relationship dynamics. Chapter 25, titled "Genetic Anxiety and Its Impact on Romantic Relationships," delves into the complexities of managing anxiety-related symptoms within the context of a romantic partnership influenced by genetic predisposition. This chapter explores strategies for maintaining healthy connections, fostering understanding, and promoting emotional well-being in the realm of romantic relationships.

Understanding the Interplay of Genetic Anxiety and Romantic Relationships

The chapter begins by introducing the interplay between genetic anxiety and romantic relationships. It highlights how genetic predisposition can impact individuals' experiences of anxiety within the context of intimate partnerships.

Open Communication and Vulnerability

Exploring open communication, the chapter discusses the importance of sharing anxiety-related experiences and concerns with one's partner. Transparent communication fosters understanding, empathy, and a sense of shared vulnerability.

Creating a Supportive Partner Dynamic

The chapter emphasizes the creation of a supportive partner dynamic. Partners can offer emotional support, validation, and a safe space where anxiety-related feelings can be openly expressed.

Balancing Independence and Interdependence

Exploring the balance between independence and interdependence, the chapter discusses how individuals with genetic anxiety can maintain their autonomy while still seeking emotional support from their partners.

Understanding Triggers and Emotional Cues

The chapter delves into the understanding of triggers and emotional cues within romantic relationships. Partners can learn to recognize anxiety-related cues and respond with compassion and sensitivity.

Coping Strategies as a Couple

Exploring coping strategies as a couple, the chapter discusses how partners can collaboratively develop techniques to manage anxiety-related symptoms. Shared coping strategies promote a sense of teamwork and emotional well-being.

Intimacy and Emotional Connection

The impact of intimacy and emotional connection on managing genetic anxiety is explored. Partners can foster emotional intimacy through open communication, shared experiences, and mutual support.

Respecting Personal Boundaries

The chapter emphasizes respecting personal boundaries within romantic relationships. Partners can acknowledge each other's need for space and self-care, supporting each other's well-being.

Professional Guidance and Couples Therapy

Exploring professional guidance and couples therapy, the chapter discusses how seeking therapy can provide a structured space for addressing anxiety-related challenges as a couple. Couples therapy offers tools for effective communication and conflict resolution.

Promoting Trust and Security

The chapter delves into promoting trust and security within romantic relationships. Partners can build trust through consistent emotional availability, reliability, and reassurance.

Long-Term Relationship Growth

The chapter concludes by emphasizing the potential for long-term growth within romantic relationships affected by genetic anxiety. It underscores that while genetics may influence the landscape of anxiety, couples can develop strategies that nurture emotional well-being, promote resilience, and empower both individuals to thrive despite the challenges posed by anxiety-related symptoms.

Conclusion

"Genetic Anxiety and Its Impact on Romantic Relationships" concludes by highlighting the transformative power of relationships that navigate genetic anxiety with empathy and understanding. The chapter underscores that while genetics may shape the context of anxiety, partners can create a relationship marked by emotional connection, resilience, and the ability to overcome anxiety-related obstacles together.

CHAPTER 26: OVERCOMING GENETIC ANXIETY: INSPIRATIONAL SUCCESS STORIES

Introduction

"Overcoming Genetic Anxiety: Inspirational Success Stories" is a chapter that shines a spotlight on real-life individuals who have triumphed over the challenges posed by genetic anxiety. This chapter serves as a source of inspiration, highlighting personal narratives that showcase the resilience, determination, and strategies that have enabled individuals to overcome the impact of genetic predisposition on their anxiety-related experiences.

Highlighting Diverse Journeys

The chapter begins by introducing the diverse journeys of individuals who have navigated the complexities of genetic anxiety. These stories encompass various backgrounds, ages, and life circumstances, illustrating that the experience of genetic anxiety is not limited to a specific demographic.

Sharing Personal Narratives

Through the sharing of personal narratives, the chapter delves into the unique challenges individuals have faced due to genetic anxiety. These stories candidly address moments of struggle, self-discovery, and the process of finding effective coping mechanisms.

Strategies for Success

The heart of the chapter lies in the strategies that individuals have employed to overcome genetic anxiety. These strategies encompass a wide range of approaches, from mindfulness techniques and therapy to lifestyle modifications and support systems.

Fostering Resilience

The chapter emphasizes the role of resilience in each success story. Resilience is showcased as the driving force that empowered individuals to confront anxiety-related symptoms, seek help, and actively engage in their personal growth.

Breaking Down Stigma

Many of the success stories highlight the importance of breaking down the stigma surrounding mental health and genetic anxiety. By sharing their experiences, individuals contribute to destigmatizing conversations around anxiety-related challenges.

Finding Support Networks

The chapter underscores the significance of finding support networks. Success stories often feature the role of friends, family, partners, therapists, and support groups in providing a safety net and validation for individuals facing genetic anxiety.

Triumphs and Milestones

Triumphs and milestones are celebrated within each success story. These accomplishments showcase how individuals have managed to lead fulfilling lives, pursue their goals, and maintain emotional well-being despite genetic anxiety.

Personal Growth and Transformation

The transformative power of personal growth is a recurring theme in each narrative. Individuals share how overcoming genetic anxiety has led to increased self-awareness, emotional intelligence, and a deeper connection with themselves and others.

Inspiration and Hope

"Overcoming Genetic Anxiety: Inspirational Success Stories" concludes by highlighting the inspiration and hope that these narratives offer. The chapter underscores that while genetic anxiety presents challenges, individuals have the capacity to cultivate resilience, seek support, and carve out a path to success, happiness, and well-being.

Conclusion

The "Overcoming Genetic Anxiety: Inspirational Success Stories" chapter serves as a testament to the human spirit's capacity for growth, adaptation, and triumph. By showcasing real-life individuals who have conquered the hurdles of genetic anxiety, the chapter instills hope, provides practical insights, and reinforces the message that overcoming anxiety-related challenges is possible with the right strategies, support, and mindset.

CHAPTER 27: GENETIC ANXIETY IN THE DIGITAL AGE: CHALLENGES AND SOLUTIONS

Introduction

"Genetic Anxiety in the Digital Age: Challenges and Solutions" addresses the unique ways in which the digital era impacts individuals with genetic anxiety. This chapter delves into the potential triggers and stressors of modern technology, social media, and online interactions, and explores strategies to navigate these challenges while maintaining emotional well-being.

Understanding Digital Age and Anxiety

The chapter begins by introducing the concept of genetic anxiety within the context of the digital age. It highlights how technology and online interactions can exacerbate anxiety-related symptoms for individuals who are genetically predisposed.

Digital Triggers and Comparison Culture

Exploring digital triggers, the chapter discusses how constant connectivity and exposure to idealized online personas can contribute to anxiety. The comparison culture fueled by social media can amplify feelings of inadequacy and self-doubt.

Information Overload and Decision Fatigue

The impact of information overload and decision fatigue on anxiety is explored. The influx of information and choices in the digital age can overwhelm individuals and contribute to heightened anxiety responses.

Fear of Missing Out (FOMO) and Anxiety

The chapter delves into the relationship between the Fear of Missing Out (FOMO) and anxiety. The pressure to stay updated and connected can intensify feelings of anxiety and a sense of being left out.

Cyberbullying and Online Harassment

Exploring cyberbullying and online harassment, the chapter discusses how negative online experiences can contribute to anxiety. Individuals with genetic anxiety may be more vulnerable to the emotional impact of online negativity.

Strategies for Digital Well-being

The heart of the chapter lies in strategies for digital well-being. These strategies include setting boundaries for technology use, cultivating a positive online environment, and engaging in digital detoxes.

Mindful Social Media Consumption

The chapter emphasizes the importance of mindful social media consumption. Practicing intentionality while using social media platforms can reduce comparison-related anxiety and promote emotional well-being.

Digital Self-Care and Mental Health Apps

Exploring digital self-care, the chapter discusses the role of mental health apps and online resources. These tools can provide support, coping strategies, and relaxation techniques tailored to individuals dealing with genetic anxiety.

Building Digital Resilience

The chapter underscores the importance of building digital resilience. Learning to manage negative online interactions, setting privacy settings, and developing a critical online perspective can enhance emotional strength.

Balancing Online and Offline Interactions

Exploring the balance between online and offline interactions, the chapter discusses the importance of fostering real-life connections. Face-to-face interactions can counteract the isolating effects of excessive digital engagement.

Technology-Assisted Therapies

The chapter delves into technology-assisted therapies. Virtual therapy sessions, chatbots, and online support groups can offer individuals with genetic anxiety accessible and convenient avenues for seeking help.

Digital Literacy and Education

The chapter concludes by emphasizing the significance of digital literacy and education. Individuals can empower themselves by becoming informed about the potential risks and benefits of technology, allowing them to navigate the digital age more effectively.

Conclusion

"Genetic Anxiety in the Digital Age: Challenges and Solutions" concludes by highlighting the transformative potential of navigating the digital landscape with awareness and intentionality. The chapter underscores that while genetics may influence anxiety responses, individuals can employ strategies to harness the benefits of technology while mitigating its negative impact, ultimately leading to a digital experience marked by well-being, balance, and emotional strength.

CHAPTER 28: GENETICS, TRAUMA, AND ANXIETY: UNTANGLING THE CONNECTION

Introduction

"Genetics, Trauma, and Anxiety: Untangling the Connection" delves into the intricate relationship between genetic predisposition, trauma, and anxiety. This chapter explores how genetic factors interact with traumatic experiences to shape anxiety responses, offering insights into the complex interplay and potential strategies for managing anxiety in individuals who have experienced trauma.

Understanding the Intersection

The chapter begins by introducing the intersection of genetics, trauma, and anxiety. It underscores how genetic predisposition and traumatic events can interact to heighten vulnerability to anxiety-related symptoms.

Genetic Sensitivity to Trauma

Exploring genetic sensitivity to trauma, the chapter discusses how certain genetic traits may influence an individual's response to traumatic events. Genetic factors can impact resilience and coping mechanisms in the aftermath of trauma.

Trauma-Related Anxiety Responses

The impact of trauma on anxiety responses is explored. Genetic predisposition can contribute to the development of specific anxiety disorders, such as post-traumatic stress disorder (PTSD), following traumatic experiences.

Epigenetics and Trauma

The chapter delves into epigenetics and its role in the

connection between genetics, trauma, and anxiety. Epigenetic changes, influenced by trauma, can modulate gene expression and affect anxiety-related pathways.

Resilience and Genetic Factors

Exploring resilience, the chapter discusses how genetic factors influence an individual's ability to cope with trauma. Genetic predisposition can either enhance or hinder an individual's capacity to recover from traumatic experiences.

Trauma-Informed Approaches to Anxiety Management

The heart of the chapter lies in trauma-informed approaches to anxiety management. These approaches recognize the role of trauma in shaping anxiety responses and offer strategies to address both genetic predisposition and traumatic experiences.

Cognitive-Behavioral Therapies for Trauma-Related Anxiety

The chapter emphasizes the effectiveness of cognitive-behavioral therapies tailored to trauma-related anxiety. These therapies address negative thought patterns, promote emotional regulation, and equip individuals with coping skills.

Supporting Genetic Resilience After Trauma

Exploring genetic resilience after trauma, the chapter discusses how individuals can harness their genetic predisposition for resilience. Engaging in self-care, seeking support, and practicing coping strategies can enhance emotional strength.

Intergenerational Trauma and Genetics

The chapter delves into intergenerational trauma and its genetic implications. Traumatic experiences in one generation can impact gene expression and potentially influence anxiety responses in subsequent generations.

Holistic Approaches to Trauma and Anxiety

The chapter discusses holistic approaches to managing trauma-related anxiety. Mindfulness, yoga, art therapy, and other holistic practices can support emotional healing and well-being.

Personalized Treatment Plans

The chapter concludes by emphasizing the significance of personalized treatment plans for individuals dealing with genetics, trauma, and anxiety. Tailored interventions consider an individual's genetic predisposition, trauma history, and specific anxiety-related symptoms.

Conclusion

"Genetics, Trauma, and Anxiety: Untangling the Connection" concludes by highlighting the transformative potential of understanding the complex relationship between genetics, trauma, and anxiety. The chapter underscores that while genetics and trauma can shape anxiety responses, individuals can employ targeted strategies that promote healing, resilience, and the ability to navigate anxiety-related challenges with strength and self-awareness.

CHAPTER 29: EPIGENETICS: HOW LIFESTYLE INFLUENCES GENETIC ANXIETY EXPRESSION

Introduction

"Epigenetics: How Lifestyle Influences Genetic Anxiety Expression" delves into the fascinating realm of epigenetics, exploring how lifestyle factors interact with genetic predisposition to influence the expression of anxiety-related traits. This chapter unravels the intricate connection between genetics, environment, and lifestyle choices, shedding light on how individuals can modulate their genetic predisposition to anxiety through conscious lifestyle modifications.

Understanding Epigenetics and Genetic Expression

The chapter begins by introducing the concept of epigenetics, highlighting how environmental factors can modify gene expression without altering the DNA sequence. It underscores the role of epigenetics in shaping anxiety-related tendencies.

Gene-Environment Interaction and Anxiety

Exploring gene-environment interaction, the chapter discusses how lifestyle choices interact with genetic predisposition to impact anxiety expression. Environmental factors can either enhance or mitigate anxiety-related traits.

Diet and Nutritional Influences

The impact of diet and nutrition on genetic anxiety expression is explored. Nutrient intake can influence epigenetic modifications that affect neurotransmitter balance and brain health, contributing to anxiety-related symptoms.

Exercise and Physical Activity

Exploring exercise and physical activity, the chapter discusses how regular movement can modulate gene expression. Exercise promotes the release of neurotransmitters and endorphins that counteract anxiety-related responses.

Sleep Quality and Genetic Predisposition

The chapter delves into the relationship between sleep quality and genetic predisposition to anxiety. Adequate sleep supports genetic resilience and emotional regulation, while sleep disturbances can amplify anxiety-related symptoms.

Stress Management and Epigenetic Changes

Exploring stress management, the chapter discusses how mindfulness, relaxation techniques, and stress-reduction practices can induce epigenetic changes that alleviate anxiety-related gene expression.

Mind-Body Practices and Genetic Resilience

The heart of the chapter lies in mind-body practices that influence genetic resilience. Meditation, yoga, and deep breathing can promote relaxation, modulate gene expression, and counteract anxiety tendencies.

Social Connections and Genetic Impact

Exploring social connections, the chapter discusses how supportive relationships can impact gene expression. Positive social interactions promote emotional well-being and potentially mitigate anxiety-related genetic expression.

Environmental Toxins and Epigenetic Effects

The chapter delves into the impact of environmental toxins on epigenetics and anxiety expression. Exposure to pollutants and toxins can lead to epigenetic changes that influence anxiety-related traits.

Positive Lifestyle Changes for Anxiety

The chapter emphasizes positive lifestyle changes for managing anxiety. By adopting a balanced diet, engaging in regular exercise, prioritizing sleep, and practicing stress reduction, individuals can optimize their genetic predisposition.

Personalized Lifestyle Strategies

Exploring personalized strategies, the chapter discusses the importance of tailoring lifestyle choices to an individual's genetic profile. Genetic testing can offer insights that guide lifestyle modifications for anxiety management.

Conclusion

"**Epigenetics: How Lifestyle Influences Genetic Anxiety Expression**" concludes by highlighting the transformative potential of lifestyle choices in shaping anxiety-related gene expression. The chapter underscores that while genetics may play a role in anxiety, individuals have the agency to modulate their genetic predisposition through mindful lifestyle modifications, ultimately leading to a life marked by well-being, resilience, and the ability to thrive despite anxiety-related challenges.

CHAPTER 30: PREVENTING GENETIC ANXIETY: A FOCUS ON EARLY INTERVENTION

Introduction

"Preventing Genetic Anxiety: A Focus on Early Intervention" explores the proactive strategies and interventions that can mitigate the impact of genetic predisposition to anxiety from an early age. This chapter highlights the importance of recognizing signs, providing support, and implementing preventive measures to promote emotional well-being and resilience in individuals at risk of developing genetic anxiety.

Understanding Early Intervention in Genetic Anxiety

The chapter begins by introducing the concept of early intervention in the context of genetic anxiety. It underscores the significance of identifying genetic predisposition and anxiety-related traits in individuals at a young age.

Identifying Genetic Risk Factors

Exploring the identification of genetic risk factors, the chapter discusses the role of genetic testing and family history in recognizing individuals who may be susceptible to anxiety-related tendencies.

Early Signs and Symptoms

The impact of recognizing early signs and symptoms of anxiety in at-risk individuals is explored. Identifying behaviors such as excessive worrying, avoidance, and physical symptoms can pave the way for timely intervention.

Educational Programs for Children and Parents

The chapter delves into the role of educational programs for both children and parents. Age-appropriate programs can equip children with emotional coping skills, while parent-focused programs provide guidance on supporting anxious children.

Promoting Emotional Intelligence

Exploring the promotion of emotional intelligence, the chapter discusses how early intervention can foster emotional awareness and regulation. Teaching children to identify and manage their emotions can reduce the impact of genetic predisposition.

Cognitive-Behavioral Techniques for Children

The heart of the chapter lies in cognitive-behavioral techniques tailored to children. These techniques address anxious thought patterns and provide practical tools for managing anxiety-related symptoms.

School-Based Mental Health Support

The chapter emphasizes the importance of school-based mental health support. Counselors, teachers, and educators play a pivotal role in identifying and providing resources for children at risk of developing genetic anxiety.

Parental Support and Communication

Exploring parental support, the chapter discusses the significance of open communication between parents and children. Parents can create an environment where children feel comfortable discussing their feelings and concerns.

Mindfulness and Relaxation Practices

The impact of mindfulness and relaxation practices on early intervention is explored. Introducing mindfulness techniques to children can enhance their emotional regulation and resilience.

Holistic Approaches to Prevention

The chapter delves into holistic approaches to preventing genetic anxiety. Nutritional awareness, physical activity, creative outlets, and positive social interactions contribute to emotional well-being.

Early Intervention for Genetic Resilience

Exploring early intervention for genetic resilience, the chapter discusses how building resilience skills from a young age can mitigate the impact of genetic predisposition.

Conclusion

"Preventing Genetic Anxiety: A Focus on Early Intervention" concludes by highlighting the transformative potential of early intervention strategies. The chapter underscores that while genetic predisposition may influence anxiety responses, early identification and targeted interventions can empower individuals to build resilience, develop emotional tools, and lead a life marked by emotional well-being despite their genetic risk.

CHAPTER 31: GENETIC ANXIETY ACROSS GENERATIONS: BREAKING THE CYCLE

Introduction

"Genetic Anxiety Across Generations: Breaking the Cycle" delves into the intergenerational impact of genetic anxiety and explores strategies to break the cycle of anxiety transmission from one generation to the next. This chapter highlights the importance of awareness, open communication, and proactive interventions to prevent the perpetuation of genetic anxiety through family lines.

Understanding Intergenerational Impact of Genetic Anxiety

The chapter begins by introducing the concept of intergenerational impact in the context of genetic anxiety. It underscores how anxiety-related tendencies can be passed down from parents to children through both genetic and environmental factors.

Family Patterns and Communication

Exploring family patterns and communication, the chapter discusses how open conversations about anxiety within the family can lead to increased awareness and understanding of genetic predisposition.

Breaking Stigmatization and Silence

The impact of breaking stigmatization and silence surrounding mental health is explored. Encouraging open dialogue reduces shame and empowers individuals to seek help for anxiety-related symptoms.

Recognizing Early Signs in Children

The chapter delves into recognizing early signs of anxiety in children. Parents and caregivers can be vigilant about identifying anxiety-related behaviors and providing support when needed.

Parenting Strategies for Anxiety Prevention

Exploring parenting strategies, the chapter discusses how parents can implement techniques to prevent anxiety transmission. Teaching emotional coping skills, promoting resilience, and offering a supportive environment are key.

Mindful Modeling of Coping Mechanisms

The heart of the chapter lies in mindful modeling of coping mechanisms. Parents who demonstrate healthy ways of managing anxiety set positive examples for their children to emulate.

Providing Safe Spaces for Expression

The chapter emphasizes the importance of providing safe spaces for children to express their feelings and concerns about anxiety. An open and empathetic environment reduces anxiety-related isolation.

Generation-Spanning Coping Strategies

Exploring generation-spanning coping strategies, the chapter discusses how individuals can learn from the experiences of their ancestors and adopt effective anxiety management techniques.

Supporting Adolescents in Breaking the Cycle

The chapter delves into supporting adolescents in breaking the cycle of genetic anxiety. Adolescents can be empowered to recognize their genetic predisposition and engage in strategies that foster resilience.

Breaking Patterns Through Professional Help

The chapter discusses the role of professional help in breaking the cycle of genetic anxiety. Therapy and counseling offer tools for individuals and families to address anxiety-related challenges.

Creating New Narratives of Resilience

The chapter concludes by emphasizing the creation of new narratives of resilience within families. By acknowledging the presence of genetic anxiety and actively engaging in prevention strategies, families can rewrite their anxiety-related stories.

Conclusion

"Genetic Anxiety Across Generations: Breaking the Cycle" concludes by highlighting the transformative potential of breaking the cycle of genetic anxiety transmission. The chapter underscores that while genetics may play a role, families can create a legacy of emotional well-being, resilience, and empowerment, ultimately leading to a future marked by strength and the ability to thrive despite anxiety-related challenges.

CHAPTER 32: RESILIENCE-BUILDING FOR FAMILIES AFFECTED BY GENETIC ANXIETY

Introduction

"Resilience-Building for Families Affected by Genetic Anxiety" delves into the concept of resilience within families dealing with genetic anxiety. This chapter explores strategies that families can employ to foster emotional strength, effective coping, and a supportive environment in the face of genetic predisposition to anxiety.

Understanding Resilience in the Context of Genetic Anxiety

The chapter begins by introducing the concept of resilience and its relevance in the context of genetic anxiety. It underscores how resilience can empower families to navigate anxiety-related challenges with strength and adaptability.

Fostering Open Communication

Exploring fostering open communication, the chapter discusses the importance of creating a safe space where family members can openly discuss their anxiety-related experiences and concerns.

Building Emotional Coping Skills

The impact of building emotional coping skills is explored. Family members can collaborate to develop strategies that enhance emotional regulation, self-awareness, and self-compassion.

Promoting Mutual Support

The chapter delves into the significance of mutual support within families. Family members can provide validation, empathy, and encouragement to each other as they navigate their genetic predisposition to anxiety.

Creating Resilient Family Routines

Exploring resilient family routines, the chapter discusses how consistent routines and rituals can provide stability and a sense of predictability, which can be especially beneficial for individuals with genetic anxiety.

Strengthening Family Bonds

The chapter emphasizes strengthening family bonds as a means of building resilience. Engaging in shared activities, spending quality time together, and fostering a sense of belonging can enhance emotional well-being.

Positive Parenting Approaches

Exploring positive parenting approaches, the chapter discusses how parents can model and teach resilience to their children. By emphasizing problem-solving, adaptability, and a growth mindset, parents foster resilience skills.

Supporting Individual Growth

The chapter discusses the importance of supporting individual growth within the family. Encouraging family members to pursue their interests, set goals, and explore their strengths contributes to overall resilience.

Seeking Professional Help

The role of seeking professional help is explored. Family therapy, counseling, and support groups can offer specialized guidance and interventions for families dealing with genetic anxiety.

Resilience-Building Activities

The chapter delves into resilience-building activities that families can engage in. Mindfulness practices, creative outlets, and outdoor activities can enhance emotional well-being and promote connection.

Creating Resilient Narratives

The chapter concludes by emphasizing the creation of resilient narratives within families. By reframing their anxiety-related experiences and focusing on strengths, families can develop a collective identity of resilience.

Conclusion

"Resilience-Building for Families Affected by Genetic Anxiety" concludes by highlighting the transformative potential of resilience-building strategies within families. The chapter underscores that while genetics may influence anxiety responses, families can create a foundation of emotional strength, effective coping, and mutual support that empowers them to face anxiety-related challenges with resilience, unity, and the ability to thrive despite their genetic predisposition.

CHAPTER 33: CULTURAL PERSPECTIVES ON GENETIC ANXIETY AND COPING

Introduction

"Cultural Perspectives on Genetic Anxiety and Coping" explores how different cultural backgrounds influence the experience of genetic anxiety and the coping mechanisms employed by individuals and families. This chapter delves into the complexities of how cultural norms, beliefs, and practices shape the expression of anxiety-related symptoms and the strategies used to manage them.

Understanding Cultural Diversity in Anxiety Expression

The chapter begins by introducing the concept of cultural diversity in the expression of genetic anxiety. It underscores how cultural factors can influence the perception, interpretation, and communication of anxiety-related experiences.

Cultural Variations in Expressing Anxiety

Exploring cultural variations, the chapter discusses how anxiety may be expressed differently across cultures. Some cultures may emphasize physical symptoms, while others may emphasize emotional or social manifestations of anxiety.

Cultural Stigma and Mental Health

The impact of cultural stigma surrounding mental health is explored. Certain cultures may stigmatize discussing anxiety-related issues, making it challenging for individuals to seek support.

Traditional Healing Practices and Coping

Exploring traditional healing practices, the chapter discusses how cultural beliefs may lead individuals to turn to traditional remedies, rituals, and spiritual practices for managing anxiety-related symptoms.

Collectivism and Social Support

The chapter delves into how cultural collectivism influences coping with genetic anxiety. Close-knit communities may provide strong social support, which can mitigate the impact of anxiety-related challenges.

Cultural Identity and Resilience

Exploring the role of cultural identity, the chapter discusses how individuals may draw strength from their cultural heritage as a way to cope with anxiety-related symptoms.

Cultural Barriers to Seeking Help

The chapter emphasizes the importance of understanding cultural barriers to seeking professional help. Cultural norms may influence whether individuals feel comfortable accessing therapy or counseling.

Cross-Cultural Interventions

Exploring cross-cultural interventions, the chapter discusses the significance of tailoring therapeutic approaches to individuals' cultural backgrounds to ensure effectiveness.

Integration of Cultural Practices and Modern Techniques

The chapter delves into how individuals may integrate cultural practices with modern techniques for anxiety management, creating a holistic approach that aligns with their cultural values.

Cultural Sensitivity in Therapy

The chapter underscores the importance of cultural sensitivity in therapy. Therapists who are attuned to cultural nuances can provide more effective support to individuals with genetic anxiety.

Promoting Cultural Dialogue

The chapter concludes by highlighting the transformative potential of promoting cultural dialogue around genetic anxiety. Open conversations can reduce stigma, increase awareness, and foster a more inclusive approach to anxiety management.

Conclusion

"**Cultural Perspectives on Genetic Anxiety and Coping**" concludes by emphasizing the significance of cultural diversity in understanding and addressing genetic anxiety. The chapter underscores that while genetics may shape anxiety responses, cultural perspectives play a crucial role in determining how anxiety is experienced, expressed, and managed. By acknowledging and respecting cultural differences, individuals and communities can create a more inclusive and empathetic approach to anxiety-related challenges.

CHAPTER 34: THE SCIENCE OF EPIGENETICS: HARNESSING POSITIVE CHANGES

Introduction

"The Science of Epigenetics: Harnessing Positive Changes" delves into the transformative potential of epigenetics in shaping anxiety-related responses. This chapter explores how understanding the science of epigenetics can empower individuals to make positive lifestyle changes that modulate genetic predisposition, leading to improved emotional well-being and resilience.

Exploring the Science of Epigenetics

The chapter begins by introducing the science of epigenetics and its role in genetic expression. It underscores how epigenetic modifications can be influenced by environmental factors, offering opportunities for positive changes.

Epigenetics and Emotional Regulation

Exploring the connection between epigenetics and emotional regulation, the chapter discusses how lifestyle choices can influence gene expression to promote emotional resilience and well-being.

Nutrition and Epigenetic Changes

The impact of nutrition on epigenetic changes is explored. Nutrient-rich diets can influence epigenetic modifications that support brain health and mitigate anxiety-related responses.

Physical Activity and Epigenetic Modulation

Exploring physical activity, the chapter discusses how regular exercise can induce epigenetic changes that enhance neurotransmitter balance, mood regulation, and stress management.

Sleep Hygiene and Epigenetic Benefits

The chapter delves into the relationship between sleep hygiene and epigenetic benefits. Prioritizing adequate sleep supports genetic resilience and emotional well-being.

Mindfulness and Epigenetic Influence

Exploring mindfulness practices, the chapter discusses how techniques such as meditation and deep breathing can induce epigenetic changes that alleviate anxiety-related tendencies.

Social Connections and Epigenetic Impact

The impact of social connections on epigenetic modifications is explored. Positive relationships can trigger epigenetic changes that enhance emotional resilience and coping mechanisms.

Epigenetics and Cognitive Restructuring

Exploring cognitive restructuring, the chapter discusses how individuals can use cognitive-behavioral techniques to induce epigenetic changes that promote more adaptive thought patterns.

Holistic Approaches to Epigenetic Modulation

The chapter delves into holistic approaches to epigenetic modulation. Engaging in creative activities, spending time in nature, and engaging in relaxation practices can positively influence gene expression.

Personalized Epigenetic Strategies

Exploring personalized strategies, the chapter discusses the importance of tailoring lifestyle modifications to an individual's genetic profile for maximum epigenetic benefits.

Promoting Emotional Resilience

The chapter concludes by highlighting the transformative potential of harnessing epigenetic changes for emotional resilience. The chapter underscores that while genetics may influence anxiety responses, individuals can actively engage in lifestyle changes that empower them to shape their genetic expression, leading to enhanced emotional well-being, adaptive coping, and the ability to thrive despite anxiety-related challenges.

Conclusion

"The Science of Epigenetics: Harnessing Positive Changes" concludes by emphasizing the power of leveraging epigenetics to promote emotional well-being. The chapter underscores that by making informed lifestyle choices, individuals can actively mold their genetic expression in ways that counteract anxiety-related tendencies, fostering resilience, and creating a future marked by strength and the capacity to thrive.

CHAPTER 35: FROM VULNERABILITY TO STRENGTH: PERSONAL GROWTH WITH GENETIC ANXIETY

Introduction

"From Vulnerability to Strength: Personal Growth with Genetic Anxiety" explores the transformative journey of individuals who have navigated the challenges of genetic anxiety and emerged stronger and more resilient. This chapter delves into the process of personal growth, highlighting how individuals can harness their genetic predisposition to anxiety as a catalyst for positive change and empowerment.

Embracing Vulnerability and Resilience

The chapter begins by introducing the concept of vulnerability and resilience in the context of genetic anxiety. It underscores that vulnerability does not equate to weakness and can, in fact, be a foundation for cultivating strength.

Self-Discovery and Awareness

Exploring self-discovery and awareness, the chapter discusses how individuals with genetic anxiety can embark on a journey of understanding their triggers, thought patterns, and coping mechanisms.

Building Emotional Intelligence

The impact of building emotional intelligence is explored. Individuals can develop a deeper understanding of their emotions, which can aid in managing anxiety-related responses.

Mindset Shift: From Victim to Survivor

The chapter delves into the transformative mindset shift from viewing oneself as a victim of genetic anxiety to adopting the identity of a survivor who actively engages in strategies for growth and well-being.

Cultivating Coping Strategies

Exploring coping strategies, the chapter discusses how individuals can develop a toolbox of techniques that empower them to manage anxiety-related symptoms effectively.

Personal Values and Meaning

The chapter emphasizes the role of personal values and meaning in shaping the experience of genetic anxiety. By aligning actions with values, individuals can find purpose and strength in their journey.

Turning Adversity into Motivation

Exploring turning adversity into motivation, the chapter discusses how individuals can channel their experiences with genetic anxiety into a driving force for personal growth and positive change.

Harnessing Support Networks

The chapter underscores the importance of harnessing support networks. Friends, family, therapists, and support groups can provide validation, guidance, and encouragement.

Creative Expression as Healing

Exploring creative expression, the chapter discusses how engaging in artistic pursuits can provide an outlet for emotions and contribute to emotional healing.

Thriving Beyond Genetic Anxiety

The heart of the chapter lies in thriving beyond genetic anxiety. Individuals can cultivate a sense of agency, pursue their passions, and lead fulfilling lives despite their genetic predisposition.

Contributing to Mental Health Advocacy

The chapter delves into the potential for individuals to contribute to mental health advocacy. Sharing their personal stories can reduce stigma and inspire others facing genetic anxiety.

Conclusion: A Journey of Empowerment

"From Vulnerability to Strength: Personal Growth with Genetic Anxiety" concludes by highlighting the transformative potential of personal growth. The chapter underscores that while genetics may influence anxiety responses, individuals have the capacity to shape their narrative, turning vulnerability into strength and fostering a future marked by resilience, empowerment, and the ability to thrive despite anxiety-related challenges.

CHAPTER 36: ART THERAPY AND CREATIVE EXPRESSION IN MANAGING ANXIETY

Introduction

"Art Therapy and Creative Expression in Managing Anxiety" explores the therapeutic potential of art and creative expression as tools for managing anxiety-related symptoms. This chapter delves into how engaging in artistic practices can provide a unique avenue for emotional healing, self-discovery, and stress reduction, particularly in the context of genetic anxiety.

Understanding the Healing Power of Art

The chapter begins by introducing the healing power of art and creative expression. It underscores how art can serve as a nonverbal outlet for emotions and offer a means of processing complex feelings.

Art Therapy and Anxiety Management

Exploring art therapy, the chapter discusses how trained professionals can guide individuals in using various artistic mediums to explore their anxiety-related experiences and promote emotional well-being.

Visual Expression of Emotions

The impact of visual expression of emotions is explored. Art allows individuals to externalize their inner feelings, providing a tangible representation of their anxiety-related struggles.

Art as a Mindfulness Practice

The chapter delves into how engaging in art can function as a mindfulness practice. Immersed in the creative process, individuals can experience a state of flow that promotes relaxation and focus.

The Role of Creative Exploration

Exploring creative exploration, the chapter discusses how experimenting with different artistic techniques can foster self-discovery and help individuals gain insights into their anxiety-related triggers.

Art as Emotional Release

The chapter underscores how art can serve as an emotional release valve. The act of creating can provide catharsis and relief from anxiety-related tensions.

Symbolism and Self-Understanding

Exploring symbolism, the chapter discusses how individuals can use art to create symbols that represent their anxiety-related experiences, enabling deeper self-understanding.

Group Art Therapy and Community Support

The chapter emphasizes the role of group art therapy in creating a supportive community. Sharing art with others can reduce feelings of isolation and enhance a sense of connection.

Artistic Practices Beyond Therapy

Exploring artistic practices beyond therapy, the chapter discusses how individuals can integrate art into their daily lives as a form of self-care and stress reduction.

Art-Based Coping Strategies

The heart of the chapter lies in art-based coping strategies. Creating art can provide individuals with a healthy outlet for managing anxiety-related symptoms and promoting emotional well-being.

Building a Creative Toolkit

The chapter delves into building a creative toolkit for anxiety management. By exploring various artistic mediums, individuals can discover which forms of expression resonate most with them.

Conclusion: Painting a Path to Emotional Well-Being

"Art Therapy and Creative Expression in Managing Anxiety" concludes by highlighting the transformative potential of art in managing anxiety. The chapter underscores that while genetics may influence anxiety responses, engaging in creative expression provides individuals with a unique and empowering means to navigate their anxiety-related challenges, fostering emotional healing, self-discovery, and the ability to thrive despite their genetic predisposition.

CHAPTER 37: BUILDING EMOTIONAL INTELLIGENCE TO COUNTER GENETIC ANXIETY

Introduction

"Building Emotional Intelligence to Counter Genetic Anxiety" explores the role of emotional intelligence in mitigating the impact of genetic predisposition to anxiety. This chapter delves into how enhancing emotional awareness, regulation, and interpersonal skills can empower individuals to effectively manage anxiety-related symptoms and promote overall well-being.

Understanding Emotional Intelligence

The chapter begins by introducing the concept of emotional intelligence and its relevance in the context of genetic anxiety. It underscores how emotional intelligence contributes to adaptive coping and resilience.

Emotional Awareness and Self-Understanding

Exploring emotional awareness, the chapter discusses how individuals can learn to identify and understand their emotional responses, which is crucial for managing anxiety-related symptoms.

Emotion Regulation Strategies

The impact of emotion regulation strategies is explored. Individuals can learn techniques to manage anxiety-triggering emotions and prevent them from escalating.

Empathy and Interpersonal Skills

The chapter delves into the role of empathy and interpersonal skills. Developing the ability to understand and connect with others can enhance social support and reduce feelings of isolation.

Effective Communication and Conflict Resolution

Exploring effective communication, the chapter discusses how improving communication skills can reduce misunderstandings and conflicts, which can contribute to anxiety-related distress.

Self-Compassion and Anxiety Management

The chapter underscores the importance of self-compassion in anxiety management. Treating oneself with kindness and understanding can counteract self-criticism and reduce anxiety-related self-judgment.

Mindful Decision-Making

Exploring mindful decision-making, the chapter discusses how individuals can make choices that align with their values and promote emotional well-being, even in the face of anxiety-related challenges.

Stress Management and Coping

The heart of the chapter lies in stress management and coping strategies. Emotional intelligence equips individuals with tools to effectively cope with stressors and prevent anxiety-related symptoms from escalating.

Social Support and Emotional Intelligence

Exploring social support, the chapter discusses how emotional intelligence enhances one's ability to seek and maintain positive social connections, which can buffer against the impact of genetic anxiety.

Empowering Children with Emotional Intelligence

The chapter delves into empowering children with emotional intelligence skills. Teaching children to recognize and manage their emotions equips them with lifelong tools for anxiety prevention.

Cultivating Resilience Through Emotional Intelligence

The chapter emphasizes the role of emotional intelligence in cultivating resilience. Individuals can use their emotional awareness and regulation skills to bounce back from anxiety-related challenges.

Conclusion: Navigating Anxiety with Emotional Wisdom

"Building Emotional Intelligence to Counter Genetic Anxiety" concludes by highlighting the transformative potential of emotional intelligence. The chapter underscores that while genetics may influence anxiety responses, individuals can cultivate emotional intelligence to navigate their anxiety-related challenges with wisdom, adaptive coping, and resilience, ultimately leading to a future marked by emotional well-being and the ability to thrive despite genetic predisposition.

CHAPTER 38: FINDING MEANING AND PURPOSE BEYOND GENETIC PREDISPOSITION

Introduction

"Finding Meaning and Purpose Beyond Genetic Predisposition" explores how individuals can navigate their genetic predisposition to anxiety by seeking meaning and purpose in their lives. This chapter delves into how discovering a sense of meaning and engaging in purpose-driven pursuits can empower individuals to overcome anxiety-related challenges and lead fulfilling lives.

Understanding the Power of Meaning and Purpose

The chapter begins by introducing the concept of meaning and purpose and their significance in the context of genetic anxiety. It underscores how having a sense of meaning can provide a framework for navigating challenges.

Discovering Personal Values and Passions

Exploring personal values and passions, the chapter discusses how identifying what matters most to individuals can guide them towards activities and pursuits that bring fulfillment.

Aligning with Core Values

The impact of aligning with core values is explored. Engaging in activities that resonate with one's values can provide a sense of purpose that counteracts anxiety-related distress.

Contributing to Others and Community

The chapter delves into the role of contributing to others and the community. Acts of kindness and service can create a sense of purpose and enhance social connections.

Setting Meaningful Goals

Exploring setting meaningful goals, the chapter discusses how individuals can create a roadmap for their lives that reflects their aspirations, driving them towards purposeful achievements.

Creating a Sense of Legacy

The chapter emphasizes the importance of creating a sense of legacy. Focusing on leaving a positive impact on the world can provide a broader perspective that counters anxiety-related preoccupations.

Mindfulness and Meaning-Making

Exploring mindfulness, the chapter discusses how being present in the moment can lead to profound insights and revelations about one's purpose and the meaning of their experiences.

Spirituality and Transcendence

The role of spirituality and transcendence is explored. Engaging in spiritual practices can offer a sense of connection to something larger than oneself, providing comfort and purpose.

Overcoming Challenges with Purpose

The heart of the chapter lies in overcoming challenges with purpose. Individuals can draw strength from their sense of meaning and purpose, allowing them to navigate anxiety-related setbacks.

Meaning-Centered Coping Strategies

Exploring meaning-centered coping strategies, the chapter discusses how individuals can use their sense of purpose to counteract anxiety-related symptoms and build resilience.

Conclusion: Charting a Purpose-Driven Path

"Finding Meaning and Purpose Beyond Genetic Predisposition" concludes by highlighting the transformative potential of seeking meaning and purpose. The chapter underscores that while genetics may influence anxiety responses, individuals can shape their lives around a sense of purpose that empowers them to navigate anxiety-related challenges with resilience, fulfillment, and the ability to thrive despite their genetic predisposition.

CHAPTER 39: SUPPORT GROUPS AND COMMUNITY RESOURCES FOR GENETIC ANXIETY

Introduction

"Support Groups and Community Resources for Genetic Anxiety" explores the invaluable role of support groups and community resources in providing a safe and empathetic space for individuals dealing with genetic anxiety. This chapter delves into how connecting with others who share similar experiences can offer validation, encouragement, and practical strategies for managing anxiety-related challenges.

Understanding the Power of Support

The chapter begins by introducing the power of support in the context of genetic anxiety. It underscores how individuals facing similar challenges can offer a unique source of understanding and validation.

Benefits of Support Groups

Exploring the benefits of support groups, the chapter discusses how these groups provide a platform for sharing experiences, exchanging coping strategies, and fostering a sense of belonging.

Peer Empowerment and Connection

The impact of peer empowerment and connection is explored. Being part of a supportive community can empower individuals to take control of their anxiety-related challenges.

Online Support Communities

The chapter delves into the significance of online support communities. These platforms provide accessibility and anonymity, allowing individuals to connect with others regardless of geographical barriers.

Shared Experiences and Validation

Exploring shared experiences and validation, the chapter discusses how hearing others' stories can normalize feelings of anxiety and reduce feelings of isolation.

Education and Resources

The chapter emphasizes the role of education and resources provided by support groups. Individuals can gain insights into anxiety management techniques, therapies, and lifestyle modifications.

Support for Families and Caregivers

Exploring support for families and caregivers, the chapter discusses how these groups can provide guidance on understanding and supporting loved ones dealing with genetic anxiety.

Professional Guidance in Support Groups

The chapter underscores the importance of professional guidance within support groups. Facilitators can provide expert insights and ensure the groups remain focused and safe.

Coping Strategies and Skill-Sharing

Exploring coping strategies, the chapter discusses how members of support groups can share practical techniques for managing anxiety-related symptoms.

Building Resilient Connections

The heart of the chapter lies in building resilient connections within support groups. Individuals can form meaningful relationships that extend beyond the group setting.

Advocacy and Awareness

Exploring advocacy and awareness, the chapter discusses how support groups can collectively raise awareness about genetic anxiety and reduce stigma.

Conclusion: United in Strength

"Support Groups and Community Resources for Genetic Anxiety" concludes by highlighting the transformative potential of support groups and community resources. The chapter underscores that while genetics may influence anxiety responses, connecting with others who understand the journey can empower individuals to manage their anxiety-related challenges with resilience, strength, and the ability to thrive despite their genetic predisposition.

CHAPTER 40: GENETIC ANXIETY AND COEXISTING MENTAL HEALTH CONDITIONS

Introduction

"Genetic Anxiety and Coexisting Mental Health Conditions" explores the intricate relationship between genetic anxiety and other coexisting mental health conditions. This chapter delves into how understanding and addressing the intersection of genetic predisposition and other mental health challenges can lead to comprehensive and effective treatment strategies.

Understanding Comorbidity

The chapter begins by introducing the concept of comorbidity —the coexistence of multiple mental health conditions in an individual. It underscores the importance of recognizing and addressing these complex interactions.

Common Coexisting Conditions

Exploring common coexisting conditions, the chapter discusses how anxiety frequently overlaps with disorders like depression, obsessive-compulsive disorder (OCD), and post-traumatic stress disorder (PTSD).

Shared Genetic Factors

The impact of shared genetic factors in coexisting conditions is explored. Genetic predisposition may contribute to the development of multiple mental health challenges.

Biological Mechanisms and Neurotransmitters

The chapter delves into the biological mechanisms underlying coexisting conditions. Genetic factors may affect neurotransmitter regulation, brain structure, and other physiological processes.

Treatment Challenges and Considerations

Exploring treatment challenges, the chapter discusses how the presence of coexisting conditions can complicate diagnosis, treatment planning, and symptom management.

Integrated Treatment Approaches

The heart of the chapter lies in integrated treatment approaches. Addressing both genetic anxiety and coexisting conditions requires a comprehensive strategy that may involve medication, therapy, and lifestyle modifications.

Therapeutic Modalities for Coexisting Conditions

Exploring therapeutic modalities, the chapter discusses how cognitive-behavioral therapy (CBT), dialectical behavior therapy (DBT), and other evidence-based approaches can effectively address both anxiety and coexisting conditions.

Medication and Dual Diagnosis

The role of medication in dual diagnosis is explored. Psychopharmacology can play a crucial role in managing symptoms of anxiety and coexisting conditions.

Holistic Approaches to Dual Diagnosis

The chapter delves into holistic approaches to dual diagnosis. Integrating mindfulness, exercise, nutrition, and social support can contribute to overall well-being.

Support Networks and Coexisting Conditions

Exploring support networks, the chapter discusses how families, friends, and support groups can play a pivotal role in providing empathy and encouragement to individuals with genetic anxiety and coexisting conditions.

Empowering Individuals Through Education

The chapter underscores the importance of educating individuals about the coexistence of mental health conditions.

Knowledge empowers individuals to seek appropriate treatment and manage their challenges.

Conclusion: A Comprehensive Approach

"Genetic Anxiety and Coexisting Mental Health Conditions" concludes by highlighting the transformative potential of a comprehensive approach. The chapter underscores that while genetics may influence anxiety responses, addressing the complexity of coexisting conditions requires tailored strategies that address each aspect of an individual's mental health, ultimately leading to improved well-being, adaptive coping, and the ability to thrive despite genetic predisposition.

CHAPTER 41: ENHANCING SELF-ESTEEM AND CONFIDENCE DESPITE GENETIC ANXIETY

Introduction

"Enhancing Self-Esteem and Confidence Despite Genetic Anxiety" explores the profound impact of self-esteem and confidence on managing genetic anxiety. This chapter delves into how individuals can cultivate a positive self-image and build inner strength, enabling them to navigate anxiety-related challenges with resilience and a sense of empowerment.

Understanding the Role of Self-Esteem

The chapter begins by introducing the concept of self-esteem and its relevance in the context of genetic anxiety. It underscores how a healthy self-esteem can act as a protective factor against the negative effects of anxiety.

The Connection Between Self-Esteem and Confidence

Exploring the connection between self-esteem and confidence, the chapter discusses how self-esteem influences an individual's belief in their abilities to cope with anxiety-related challenges.

Challenging Negative Self-Perceptions

The impact of challenging negative self-perceptions is explored. Individuals can learn to identify and reframe self-defeating thoughts that contribute to anxiety-related distress.

Self-Compassion and Self-Worth

Exploring self-compassion, the chapter discusses how treating oneself with kindness and understanding can bolster self-worth and counteract self-criticism.

Acknowledging Personal Strengths

The chapter delves into acknowledging personal strengths. Recognizing and celebrating one's abilities can enhance self-esteem and provide a foundation for coping with anxiety.

Setting and Achieving Goals

Exploring goal-setting, the chapter discusses how achieving milestones can boost self-esteem and instill a sense of accomplishment.

Mindful Self-Awareness

Exploring mindful self-awareness, the chapter discusses how individuals can cultivate a nonjudgmental awareness of their thoughts and feelings, promoting self-acceptance.

Positive Affirmations and Self-Talk

The chapter emphasizes the role of positive affirmations and self-talk. Practicing self-affirming statements can counteract negative self-beliefs.

Supportive Relationships and Self-Esteem

Exploring supportive relationships, the chapter discusses how positive interactions with friends, family, and peers can contribute to a sense of belonging and self-worth.

Body Image and Self-Esteem

The impact of body image on self-esteem is explored. Developing a healthy body image can enhance overall self-esteem and emotional well-being.

Perfectionism and Acceptance

The chapter delves into addressing perfectionism. Cultivating acceptance of oneself, imperfections and all, can promote self-esteem and reduce anxiety-related pressure.

Conclusion: Nurturing Inner Strength

"Enhancing Self-Esteem and Confidence Despite Genetic Anxiety" concludes by highlighting the transformative potential of nurturing self-esteem and confidence. The chapter underscores that while genetics may influence anxiety responses, individuals can actively cultivate a positive self-image and inner strength, enabling them to navigate anxiety-related challenges with resilience, self-assuredness, and the ability to thrive despite their genetic predisposition.

CHAPTER 42: SETTING REALISTIC GOALS ON THE PATH TO ANXIETY MANAGEMENT

Introduction

"Setting Realistic Goals on the Path to Anxiety Management" explores the importance of goal-setting in effectively managing genetic anxiety. This chapter delves into how individuals can establish meaningful and achievable goals that contribute to their emotional well-being, resilience, and overall quality of life.

Understanding the Role of Goal-Setting

The chapter begins by introducing the concept of goal-setting and its significance in the context of genetic anxiety. It underscores how setting clear and attainable goals can provide direction and motivation.

Identifying Personal Priorities

Exploring identifying personal priorities, the chapter discusses how individuals can determine what aspects of their lives they want to improve in order to manage anxiety effectively.

Creating SMART Goals

The impact of creating SMART (Specific, Measurable, Achievable, Relevant, Time-bound) goals is explored. Using this framework ensures that goals are well-defined and actionable.

Breaking Down Larger Goals

The chapter delves into breaking down larger goals into smaller, manageable steps. This approach prevents overwhelm and provides a sense of accomplishment along the way.

Aligning Goals with Values

Exploring aligning goals with values, the chapter discusses how setting goals that resonate with personal values can foster a deeper sense of purpose and motivation.

Anxiety-Specific Goals

The chapter emphasizes the importance of setting anxiety-specific goals. These goals address anxiety-related challenges and contribute to improved emotional well-being.

Monitoring Progress and Adjusting Goals

Exploring progress monitoring, the chapter discusses how regularly assessing one's progress and adjusting goals as needed can ensure continued motivation and adaptability.

Celebrate Milestones and Achievements

The chapter underscores the significance of celebrating milestones and achievements. Recognizing progress boosts self-esteem and reinforces the value of goal-setting.

Setting Realistic Expectations

Exploring setting realistic expectations, the chapter discusses how individuals can avoid setting themselves up for disappointment by choosing goals that are achievable within their current circumstances.

Cultivating Flexibility and Adaptability

The chapter delves into cultivating flexibility and adaptability. Being open to adjusting goals in response to changing circumstances promotes resilience and reduces anxiety-related pressure.

Creating a Supportive Environment

Exploring creating a supportive environment, the chapter discusses how involving friends, family, or therapists in goal-setting can provide accountability and encouragement.

Conclusion: Forging a Path of Growth

"Setting Realistic Goals on the Path to Anxiety Management" concludes by highlighting the transformative potential of goal-setting. The chapter underscores that while genetics may influence anxiety responses, individuals can actively shape their journey by setting meaningful goals that lead to improved emotional well-being, adaptive coping, and the ability to thrive despite their genetic predisposition.

CHAPTER 43: GENETICS, GENDER, AND ANXIETY: NAVIGATING UNIQUE CHALLENGES

Introduction

"Genetics, Gender, and Anxiety: Navigating Unique Challenges" explores the intersection between genetics, gender, and anxiety experiences. This chapter delves into how gender-related factors, including biological differences, societal expectations, and cultural influences, interact with genetic predisposition to shape the experience of anxiety and the coping strategies used by individuals.

Understanding Gender and Anxiety

The chapter begins by introducing the concept of gender and its relevance in the context of anxiety. It underscores how societal and cultural norms can influence the expression and perception of anxiety in different genders.

Biological Factors and Gender

Exploring biological factors, the chapter discusses how hormonal differences between genders can contribute to variations in anxiety-related responses.

Societal Expectations and Gender Roles

The impact of societal expectations and gender roles is explored. Traditional gender roles can influence how anxiety is experienced and expressed.

Cultural Influences and Gendered Anxiety

The chapter delves into cultural influences on gendered anxiety experiences. Different cultures may have varying expectations and norms that affect how anxiety is perceived.

Intersectionality and Multiple Identities

Exploring intersectionality, the chapter discusses how individuals with multiple identities, such as gender and race, may experience unique challenges in managing genetic anxiety.

Gendered Coping Mechanisms

The chapter emphasizes how gender-related coping mechanisms can influence anxiety management. Men and women may adopt different strategies based on societal expectations.

Breaking Gender Stereotypes in Coping

Exploring breaking gender stereotypes in coping, the chapter discusses the importance of challenging rigid gender norms to allow individuals to choose coping strategies that align with their personal needs.

Seeking Help and Gender Bias

The chapter delves into gender bias in seeking help. Societal perceptions may influence whether individuals feel comfortable seeking therapy or support for anxiety-related challenges.

Empowering Gender-Sensitive Support

Exploring gender-sensitive support, the chapter discusses how professionals can provide inclusive and tailored assistance that acknowledges and respects the unique experiences of different genders.

Gender Identity and Anxiety

The chapter explores the experiences of individuals whose gender identity differs from their assigned sex at birth. Gender dysphoria and related challenges can intersect with genetic anxiety.

Supportive Communities for Gender-Diverse Individuals

The chapter underscores the significance of supportive communities for gender-diverse individuals. Peer support and safe spaces can contribute to resilience and well-being.

Conclusion: A Nuanced Approach

"Genetics, Gender, and Anxiety: Navigating Unique Challenges" concludes by highlighting the transformative potential of understanding the interplay between genetics, gender, and anxiety. The chapter underscores that while genetics may influence anxiety responses, acknowledging and addressing gender-related influences allows for a more nuanced and empathetic approach to anxiety management. By considering the diverse experiences of different genders, individuals can navigate their anxiety-related challenges with authenticity, strength, and the ability to thrive despite their genetic predisposition.

CHAPTER 44: BREAKING FREE FROM GENETIC ANXIETY: A STEP-BY-STEP JOURNEY

Introduction

"Breaking Free from Genetic Anxiety: A Step-by-Step Journey" takes readers on a comprehensive and empowering journey towards overcoming the grip of genetic anxiety. This chapter provides a roadmap of practical steps and strategies individuals can take to gradually build resilience, manage anxiety-related symptoms, and lead a fulfilling life despite their genetic predisposition.

Acknowledging the Starting Point

The chapter begins by encouraging individuals to acknowledge their anxiety and recognize its genetic origins. This self-awareness is the foundation for transformation.

Educating Yourself About Genetics and Anxiety

Exploring education, the chapter discusses the importance of understanding the genetic basis of anxiety. Learning about genetic influences empowers individuals to navigate their journey with informed perspective.

Seeking Professional Guidance

The impact of seeking professional guidance is explored. Consulting with therapists, psychiatrists, or genetic counselors can provide personalized insights and treatment recommendations.

Creating a Support Network

The chapter delves into the role of support networks. Building connections with friends, family, and support groups offers emotional validation and encouragement.

Setting Realistic Goals

Exploring goal-setting, the chapter discusses the importance of setting achievable goals to work towards. These goals can contribute to incremental progress and a sense of accomplishment.

Engaging in Self-Care Practices

The chapter emphasizes the significance of self-care practices. Incorporating exercise, nutrition, sleep hygiene, and mindfulness can enhance emotional well-being.

Developing Coping Strategies

Exploring coping strategies, the chapter discusses techniques such as deep breathing, grounding exercises, and cognitive restructuring that help manage anxiety-related symptoms.

Exploring Therapeutic Modalities

The chapter delves into various therapeutic modalities like cognitive-behavioral therapy (CBT), exposure therapy, and mindfulness-based interventions that can provide tools for anxiety management.

Implementing Lifestyle Modifications

The heart of the chapter lies in lifestyle modifications. Engaging in activities you enjoy, cultivating hobbies, and spending time in nature can counteract anxiety-related stress.

Mind-Body Techniques for Calm

Exploring mind-body techniques, the chapter discusses how practices like meditation, yoga, and tai chi can promote relaxation and emotional equilibrium.

Building Resilience Through Positive Thinking

The chapter underscores the power of positive thinking. Developing an optimistic outlook can reframe anxiety-related challenges as opportunities for growth.

Engaging in Continuous Learning

Exploring continuous learning, the chapter discusses how staying curious and open to new knowledge contributes to personal growth and adaptability.

Celebrating Progress and Growth

The chapter emphasizes the importance of celebrating progress and growth. Recognizing even small victories can boost self-esteem and motivation.

Conclusion: Empowerment on the Horizon

"Breaking Free from Genetic Anxiety: A Step-by-Step Journey" concludes by highlighting the transformative potential of taking deliberate steps towards anxiety management. The chapter underscores that while genetics may influence anxiety responses, individuals can actively shape their journey towards empowerment, resilience, and the ability to thrive despite their genetic predisposition. By embracing a systematic approach, individuals can break free from the constraints of genetic anxiety and forge a path of strength and well-being.

CHAPTER 45: THE FUTURE OF GENETIC RESEARCH AND ANXIETY TREATMENT

Introduction

"The Future of Genetic Research and Anxiety Treatment" delves into the exciting prospects that lie ahead in the fields of genetics and anxiety treatment. This chapter explores how ongoing advancements in genetic research, technology, and innovative treatment approaches hold the promise of revolutionizing our understanding of genetic anxiety and enhancing the effectiveness of therapeutic interventions.

Genomic Discoveries and Precision Medicine

The chapter begins by discussing how ongoing genomic research is unveiling intricate details about the genetic underpinnings of anxiety disorders. The emergence of precision medicine approaches aims to tailor treatments based on an individual's genetic makeup, leading to more personalized and effective interventions.

Unraveling Genetic Markers for Anxiety

Exploring genetic markers, the chapter discusses the identification of specific genetic variations associated with anxiety susceptibility. These markers could guide early intervention strategies and predict treatment responses.

Gene Editing and Therapeutic Innovation

The impact of gene editing techniques such as CRISPR-Cas9 is explored. These innovations hold potential for modifying genetic factors that contribute to anxiety, offering novel treatment avenues.

Neurobiological Insights and Targeted Therapies

The chapter delves into how genetic research is shedding light on the neurobiological mechanisms of anxiety. This knowledge can lead to the development of targeted therapies that address specific genetic pathways.

Predictive Genetic Testing for Anxiety

Exploring predictive genetic testing, the chapter discusses how individuals may have the option to assess their genetic predisposition to anxiety. This knowledge could empower proactive strategies for prevention and management.

Gene-Environment Interaction Studies

The chapter emphasizes the importance of gene-environment interaction studies. Understanding how genetics and environmental factors interact can refine our understanding of anxiety development and inform treatment approaches.

Virtual Reality and Digital Therapeutics

Exploring technology, the chapter discusses the role of virtual reality and digital therapeutics in anxiety treatment. These tools could provide immersive exposure therapy and real-time interventions.

Personalized Psychotherapy Approaches

The chapter delves into personalized psychotherapy approaches. Therapists could tailor their interventions based on an individual's genetic and neurobiological profile for more targeted outcomes.

Ethical Considerations and Genetic Counseling

Exploring ethics, the chapter discusses the importance of ethical considerations in genetic research and treatment. Genetic counseling ensures informed decision-making for individuals seeking genetic information.

Global Collaboration in Research

The chapter underscores the significance of global collaboration in genetic research. Sharing data and insights across borders can accelerate discoveries and treatment breakthroughs.

Empowerment Through Genetic Literacy

Exploring genetic literacy, the chapter discusses how educating the public about genetics can empower individuals to make informed decisions about their mental health.

Conclusion: Shaping the Future of Anxiety Treatment

"The Future of Genetic Research and Anxiety Treatment" concludes by highlighting the transformative potential of ongoing research and innovations. The chapter underscores that while genetics may influence anxiety responses, the future holds promise for more precise, personalized, and effective treatments that empower individuals to manage their anxiety-related challenges and thrive despite their genetic predisposition.

CHAPTER 46: GENETIC ANXIETY IN AN UNCERTAIN WORLD: ADAPTING TO CHANGE

Introduction

"Genetic Anxiety in an Uncertain World: Adapting to Change" explores the intersection between genetic anxiety and the challenges presented by an unpredictable and rapidly changing world. This chapter delves into how individuals can harness their genetic predisposition to anxiety as a catalyst for developing resilience, adaptability, and coping strategies that enable them to navigate uncertainty with strength and grace.

Understanding Anxiety in an Uncertain World

The chapter begins by introducing the concept of anxiety within the context of an uncertain world. It underscores how the modern world's complexities can exacerbate genetic anxiety, leading to increased stress.

The Role of Genetic Predisposition in Uncertainty

Exploring the role of genetic predisposition, the chapter discusses how individuals with genetic anxiety may be more sensitive to environmental triggers, including uncertainty and change.

Developing Resilience Through Genetic Awareness

The impact of genetic awareness on resilience is explored. Recognizing one's genetic predisposition can empower individuals to develop tailored coping strategies.

Cultivating Flexibility and Adaptability

The chapter delves into cultivating flexibility and adaptability. Genetic anxiety can serve as a catalyst for honing skills that enable individuals to navigate unexpected changes.

Mindfulness in the Face of Uncertainty

Exploring mindfulness, the chapter discusses how mindfulness practices can help individuals stay present and centered amid uncertainty, reducing anxiety-related distress.

Finding Meaning in Change

The chapter emphasizes the potential for finding meaning in change. Embracing life's shifts as opportunities for growth can counteract anxiety-related feelings of loss of control.

Creating a Supportive Network

Exploring supportive networks, the chapter discusses how connections with friends, family, and support groups can provide a safety net during uncertain times.

Adapting Coping Strategies

The chapter delves into adapting coping strategies. Individuals can refine their toolkit to include techniques that specifically address anxiety triggered by uncertainty.

Fostering Hope and Positivity

Exploring hope and positivity, the chapter discusses how cultivating an optimistic outlook can buffer the impact of uncertainty on anxiety-related symptoms.

Seeking Professional Guidance

The chapter underscores the importance of seeking professional guidance when facing uncertainty-related anxiety. Therapists can provide strategies to manage symptoms effectively.

Embracing Change as Growth

The heart of the chapter lies in embracing change as an opportunity for growth. Individuals can shift their perspective from anxiety-driven resistance to proactive adaptation.

Conclusion: Thriving in an Evolving World

"Genetic Anxiety in an Uncertain World: Adapting to Change" concludes by highlighting the transformative potential of embracing genetic anxiety as a means to develop resilience in the face of change. The chapter underscores that while genetics may influence anxiety responses, individuals can harness their genetic predisposition to become adept at navigating uncertainty, fostering adaptability, and thriving despite the challenges presented by an evolving world.

CHAPTER 47: WRITING YOUR GENETIC ANXIETY NARRATIVE: JOURNALING FOR HEALING

Introduction

"Writing Your Genetic Anxiety Narrative: Journaling for Healing" explores the therapeutic power of journaling as a tool for individuals dealing with genetic anxiety. This chapter delves into how the act of writing can provide an outlet for processing emotions, gaining insights, and fostering healing on the journey to managing anxiety-related challenges.

Understanding Journaling as Healing

The chapter begins by introducing the concept of journaling as a healing practice. It underscores how writing allows individuals to externalize their thoughts and emotions, creating a space for reflection and understanding.

Creating a Safe Space for Expression

Exploring the safe space journaling provides, the chapter discusses how individuals can freely express their anxiety-related thoughts without fear of judgment or misunderstanding.

Tracking Patterns and Triggers

The impact of tracking patterns and triggers through journaling is explored. Individuals can identify recurring themes, situations, and emotions that contribute to their anxiety.

Processing Emotional Experiences

The chapter delves into how journaling facilitates the processing of emotional experiences. Writing allows individuals to examine their feelings, gain perspective, and release emotional weight.

Gaining Self-Awareness and Insights

Exploring self-awareness, the chapter discusses how journaling can lead to valuable insights about one's anxiety triggers, thought patterns, and coping mechanisms.

Promoting Emotional Regulation

The chapter emphasizes how journaling promotes emotional regulation. Expressing anxious thoughts on paper can reduce their intensity and help individuals manage their emotions.

Setting Goals and Celebrating Progress

Exploring goal-setting, the chapter discusses how journaling can be used to set goals for anxiety management and celebrate milestones and achievements.

Exploring Positive Affirmations

The chapter delves into incorporating positive affirmations into journaling. Writing self-affirming statements can counteract negative self-beliefs and promote self-esteem.

Creating a Ritual of Self-Care

Exploring journaling as a self-care ritual, the chapter discusses how setting aside time for writing can become a soothing and grounding practice.

Capturing Moments of Gratitude

The chapter underscores the role of gratitude in journaling. Focusing on positive aspects of life can balance the impact of anxiety-related thoughts.

Shifting Perspectives Through Writing

The heart of the chapter lies in how writing can shift perspectives. Journaling can help individuals reframe anxiety-related challenges as opportunities for growth.

Conclusion: Your Healing Narrative

"Writing Your Genetic Anxiety Narrative: Journaling for Healing" concludes by highlighting the transformative potential of journaling. The chapter underscores that while genetics may influence anxiety responses, individuals can use the power of writing to create a healing narrative. By journaling their thoughts, feelings, and insights, individuals can navigate their anxiety-related challenges with self-awareness, clarity, and the ability to thrive despite their genetic predisposition.

CHAPTER 48: BRIDGING THE GAP: COMMUNICATION ABOUT GENETIC ANXIETY

Introduction

"Bridging the Gap: Communication About Genetic Anxiety" explores the importance of open and empathetic communication when dealing with genetic anxiety. This chapter delves into how individuals can navigate conversations with loved ones, healthcare professionals, and support networks to foster understanding, collaboration, and a shared sense of support in managing anxiety-related challenges.

Understanding the Need for Communication

The chapter begins by introducing the critical role of communication in the context of genetic anxiety. It underscores how expressing one's feelings and experiences can lead to greater emotional connection and support.

Opening Up to Loved Ones

Exploring communication with loved ones, the chapter discusses how sharing one's anxiety-related challenges with family and friends can lead to increased empathy and mutual understanding.

Educating Others About Genetic Anxiety

The impact of educating others about genetic anxiety is explored. Providing information about the genetic basis of anxiety can reduce stigma and enhance support.

Creating an Environment of Empathy

The chapter delves into how empathy can be cultivated in conversations. Active listening and validating emotions create an environment where individuals feel understood and supported.

Seeking Support Through Professional Communication

Exploring communication with healthcare professionals, the chapter discusses the importance of discussing genetic anxiety with therapists, psychiatrists, and genetic counselors to receive tailored guidance and treatment.

Navigating Difficult Conversations

The chapter emphasizes the significance of navigating difficult conversations. Addressing misunderstandings or conflicts with empathy can strengthen relationships and support systems.

Empowering Advocacy Through Communication

Exploring advocacy, the chapter discusses how open communication can empower individuals to advocate for their needs and seek appropriate resources.

Promoting Emotional Well-being Through Communication

The chapter underscores how conversations about genetic anxiety can promote emotional well-being. Sharing emotions and concerns can alleviate feelings of isolation.

Building a Support Network

Exploring communication in support networks, the chapter discusses how joining support groups or online communities can provide a platform for sharing experiences and advice.

Fostering Conversations About Genetic Anxiety in Schools and Workplaces

The chapter delves into conversations in educational and workplace settings. Advocating for understanding and accommodation can contribute to a more inclusive environment.

Creating a Blueprint for Family Communication

The heart of the chapter lies in creating a blueprint for

family communication. Establishing norms for open and non-judgmental discussions fosters a supportive atmosphere.

Conclusion: Strengthening Connections Through Communication

"Bridging the Gap: Communication About Genetic Anxiety" concludes by highlighting the transformative potential of effective communication. The chapter underscores that while genetics may influence anxiety responses, open and empathetic conversations can strengthen connections, reduce isolation, and foster a sense of shared support. By engaging in meaningful dialogues, individuals can navigate their anxiety-related challenges with a greater sense of understanding, collaboration, and the ability to thrive despite their genetic predisposition.

CHAPTER 49: CELEBRATING PROGRESS AND RESILIENCE ALONG THE WAY

Introduction

"Celebrating Progress and Resilience Along the Way" explores the importance of recognizing and commemorating achievements in the journey of managing genetic anxiety. This chapter delves into how acknowledging progress, no matter how small, and cultivating a sense of resilience can contribute to a positive outlook, increased self-esteem, and a greater ability to navigate anxiety-related challenges.

Understanding the Role of Celebration

The chapter begins by introducing the concept of celebration and its significance in the context of genetic anxiety management. It underscores how celebrating progress can act as a powerful motivator.

Acknowledging Incremental Achievements

Exploring acknowledging achievements, the chapter discusses the importance of recognizing small steps taken towards managing anxiety-related challenges.

Shifting Focus from Setbacks to Successes

The impact of shifting focus from setbacks to successes is explored. Celebrating achievements reframes the narrative from one of struggle to one of growth.

Creating a Culture of Resilience

The chapter delves into how celebrating resilience contributes to a culture of strength and adaptability in the face of genetic anxiety.

Using Milestones as Markers of Progress

Exploring milestones, the chapter discusses how using these markers of progress can provide a sense of direction and accomplishment.

Cultivating Self-Appreciation

Exploring self-appreciation, the chapter discusses how celebrating one's efforts fosters a positive self-image and nurtures self-esteem.

Recognizing Support Systems

The chapter underscores the importance of recognizing the contributions of support systems—friends, family, therapists, and support groups—in the journey.

Journaling Achievements and Moments of Triumph

Exploring journaling, the chapter discusses how recording achievements and moments of triumph provides a tangible record of progress.

Balancing Reflection and Future Focus

Exploring balance, the chapter discusses the equilibrium between reflecting on achievements and looking ahead to further growth.

Creating Personal Celebration Rituals

The heart of the chapter lies in creating personal celebration rituals. Designing rituals around achievements reinforces their significance.

Savoring the Present Moments

The chapter emphasizes the practice of savoring the present moments of progress, allowing individuals to fully embrace their growth.

Conclusion: Embracing Your Journey

"Celebrating Progress and Resilience Along the Way" concludes by highlighting the transformative potential of celebration and resilience. The chapter underscores that while genetics may influence anxiety responses, embracing progress and fostering resilience contribute to a more positive and empowered experience of managing genetic anxiety. By acknowledging achievements and cultivating strength, individuals can navigate their anxiety-related challenges with a sense of accomplishment, self-assuredness, and the ability to thrive despite their genetic predisposition.

CHAPTER 50: EMBRACING A LIFE BEYOND GENETIC ANXIETY: THRIVING IN MIND AND BODY

Introduction

"Embracing a Life Beyond Genetic Anxiety: Thriving in Mind and Body" explores the ultimate goal of transcending the constraints of genetic anxiety and living a life of holistic well-being. This chapter delves into how individuals can cultivate a balanced and fulfilling life by nurturing their mental and physical health, fostering resilience, and thriving despite their genetic predisposition.

Understanding Holistic Well-being

The chapter begins by introducing the concept of holistic well-being and its significance in the context of genetic anxiety. It underscores the interconnectedness of mental, emotional, and physical health.

Prioritizing Mental and Emotional Health

Exploring mental and emotional health, the chapter discusses the importance of seeking therapy, practicing self-care, and engaging in activities that promote emotional well-being.

Incorporating Mindfulness and Meditation

The impact of mindfulness and meditation is explored. These practices can foster inner peace, reduce anxiety, and promote overall mental clarity.

Nurturing Physical Health

The chapter delves into nurturing physical health. Engaging in regular exercise, maintaining a balanced diet, and prioritizing sleep contribute to overall well-being.

Creating a Balanced Lifestyle

Exploring a balanced lifestyle, the chapter discusses how finding equilibrium between work, social activities, and personal time promotes a sense of fulfillment.

Engaging in Passion and Purpose

The chapter emphasizes the significance of engaging in passions and purpose-driven activities. Pursuing meaningful endeavors contributes to a sense of accomplishment.

Cultivating Resilience Through Challenges

Exploring resilience, the chapter discusses how facing challenges head-on and learning from setbacks contribute to personal growth.

Forging Deep Connections

Exploring connections, the chapter discusses the importance of nurturing meaningful relationships that provide emotional support and a sense of belonging.

Living Mindfully in the Present

The chapter underscores the practice of living mindfully in the present moment. Focusing on the now reduces anxiety related to the past or future.

Exploring Creativity and Expression

Exploring creativity, the chapter discusses how engaging in creative outlets fosters self-expression and a sense of empowerment.

Continued Learning and Personal Growth

The heart of the chapter lies in continued learning. Seeking knowledge and personal growth contributes to a fulfilling and purposeful life.

Conclusion: Thriving Beyond Genetics

"Embracing a Life Beyond Genetic Anxiety: Thriving in Mind and Body" concludes by highlighting the transformative potential of embracing holistic well-being. The chapter underscores that while genetics may influence anxiety responses, individuals can transcend their genetic predisposition by nurturing their mental, emotional, and physical health. By fostering resilience, living with purpose, and nurturing positive connections, individuals can navigate their anxiety-related challenges and lead a life that is not defined by genetics, but rather by their ability to thrive and flourish.

The End.

www.ingramcontent.com/pod-product-compliance
Lightning Source LLC
Chambersburg PA
CBHW070015260726
48663CB00005B/25